THE REAL READER'S QUARTERLY

Slightly Foxed

'A Year in Barsetshire'

D1115519

NO.73   SPRING 2022

Editors: Gail Pirkis & Hazel Wood
Editorial & submissions: Anna Kirk
Marketing & publicity: Steph Allen, Jennie Harrison Bunning & Hattie Summers
Subscriptions, orders & bookshops: Jess Dalby & Iona Glen

Cover illustration: Sandra Graham, *River Rea, 2021*

Sandra Graham is a professional landscape artist whose work is in both public and private collections. *River Rea, 2021* was inspired by a glorious walk through the forest and along the river during lockdown last spring. She says: 'Everything about the forest captivates and relaxes me, and its sounds, smells and textures offer endless inspiration. My work attempts to share this experience and to encourage us to consider what we now have and what we must undoubtedly protect.' For more of her work visit www.sandragraham.co.uk or follow her on Instagram @sandragrahamartist.

Back cover fox by Robert Aspinall
Design by Octavius Murray
Layout by Andrew Evans
Colophon and tailpiece by David Eccles

Published by Slightly Foxed Limited
53 Hoxton Square
London N1 6PB

tel 020 7033 0258
email office@foxedquarterly.com
www.foxedquarterly.com

Slightly Foxed is published quarterly in early March, June, September and December

Annual subscription rates (4 issues)
UK and Ireland £48; Overseas £56

Single copies of this issue can be bought for £12.50 (UK) or £14.50 (Overseas)

All back issues in printed form are also available

ISBN 978-1-910898-64-2
ISSN 1742-5794

Printed and bound by Smith Settle, Yeadon, West Yorkshire

Contents

Contents

Clare Curtis

The Slightly Foxed Podcast

A new episode of our podcast is available on the 15th of April, July, October
and January. To listen, visit www.foxedquarterly.com/pod or search for
Slightly Foxed on Audioboom, Apple Podcasts or your podcast app.

Subscriber Benefits

Slightly Foxed can obtain any books reviewed in this issue, whether new or
second-hand. To enquire about a book, to access the digital edition of *Slightly
Foxed* or to view a list of membership benefits, visit www.foxedquarterly.com/
members or contact the office: 020 7033 0258/office@foxedquarterly.com.

From the Editors

After a long winter of disruptions, there's definitely a feeling of spring in the air at Slightly Foxed. We know we're not out of the woods yet where Covid is concerned, but the start of the year has been busy, and we're still enjoying the novelty of meeting in the office instead of facing unflattering versions of ourselves on Zoom. Outside in the square the trees are just coming into bud, and the tatty old London pigeons are bowing and flirting on the ledge outside the office window.

It all feels like an invitation to be out and doing, perhaps in the kind of countryside captured by our spring cover. It's by the landscape artist Sandra Graham, and was, she says, inspired by the many different shades of green she saw during a walk last year in the Midlands along the River Rea. We do enjoy choosing and commissioning the *SF* covers, and doing so has introduced us to artists and illustrators working in many different media, from oil and watercolour to wood engraving, lithography and mosaics.

Walking in parks and in the countryside was one of the things that made lockdown bearable for many of us, and this included our contributor Daisy Hay. On p.7 she describes the pleasure it gave her to walk in the country to the accompaniment of an audiobook reading of Trollope's Barchester novels. The year she spent among the inhabitants of that imaginary cathedral town, with their ambitions, feuds and love affairs, transported her into a world soothingly far away from the stresses of the present day.

Our spring Slightly Foxed Edition *Lark Rise* (see p.14), Flora Thompson's lightly fictionalized memoir of her rural childhood at the end of the nineteenth century, is another guaranteed de-stresser.

Flora's father was a stonemason and then a bricklayer in a tiny, poverty-stricken Oxfordshire hamlet. While most other countryside writers of the period were comfortably middle-class, this record of a vanishing world came from a writer who was part of it. As Flora's biographer Margaret Lane observed: 'She was able to write the annals of the poor because she was one of them.'

Flora educated herself by going to work for the Post Office in a nearby village, and she describes this experience in *Over to Candleford* and *Candleford Green*, which we'll be publishing as one volume this coming June and which can be pre-ordered now. The trilogy is an enduring masterpiece, acutely observed, poetic, poignant, but never sentimental. 'You are going to be loved by people you've never seen and never will see,' a gypsy tells Laura, the fictional name Flora gave herself, and that prediction turned out to be true. These lovable books will be a joy if you are reading them for the first time, and if they are already a favourite why not enjoy them again in our two lovely Slightly Foxed Editions.

And finally, the podcasts. We get so many cheering and enthusiastic messages about the podcasts and some of them ask if they could be longer. It's true that sometimes after a recording we do have a feeling there's more that could have been said, but we've been wary of bombarding you with too much too often. So we've decided on a compromise: from now on the podcasts will be longer – an hour or so – and there will be four a year rather than one a month, going out six weeks after each issue. We feel this will give us both a little more breathing space and enable us to offer you more depth and variety. The next podcast will be in mid-April so do please listen in and tell us what you think.

GAIL PIRKIS & HAZEL WOOD

A Year in Barsetshire

DAISY HAY

In the spring of 2020, amidst the early devastation of Covid-19, I found myself unable to read. I was grappling with the after-effects of an accident when the pandemic struck, so my concentration was already fractured by the time the streets fell silent. Deprived of the consolations of print, one April afternoon I pressed play on the first chapter of the audiobook of Anthony Trollope's *The Warden* as I left the house for my daily walk. I did so without much expectation that the noise would do anything other than provide a mild distraction from the exigencies of the day, but within minutes the cathedral close of Barchester had opened up before me and I was hooked. What follows is an account of the year I spent among the inhabitants of Barsetshire, and of the solace I found in the connected stories of the Barchester novels.

*

On this cloudless April afternoon, as I shut the front door of my house in Exeter, my route takes me out of town and into the Devon countryside. Multi-coloured crayon rainbows in the windows of my neighbours' houses give way as I walk to verges of bluebells and forget-me-nots; then to meadows where the first daisies and buttercups are just beginning to emerge from their hiding places in the grass. In Barchester the warden of Hiram's Hospital,

---

Anthony Trollope's six Barchester novels (*The Warden, Barchester Towers, Doctor Thorne, Framley Parsonage, The Small House at Allington* and *The Last Chronicle of Barset*), read by Timothy West, are all available to download from Audible Books: visit www.audible.co.uk.

Septimus Harding, is blissfully unaware of the trouble soon to be visited on him by the twin personages of his putative son-in-law, John Bold, and his actual son-in-law, Archdeacon Theophilus Grantly. John Bold is bent on uncovering the corruption that enables Mr Harding's comfortable sinecure as the warden of the Hospital. Archdeacon Grantly is equally determined to maintain both his father-in-law's position and the rightful order of ecclesiastical things.

The Warden tells the story of the battle between John Bold and the Archdeacon, a battle in which Mr Harding finds himself most uncomfortably entangled. Although John Bold wins the hand of Mr Harding's younger daughter, Eleanor, he is a cipher compared to the formidable figure of Archdeacon Grantly. The Archdeacon's magnificence is most fully revealed as he presides over his breakfast table at Plumstead Episcopi. Trollope's description of the 'ordinary fare' of the household at breakfast demonstrates both Grantly's determination to have and be the best in all things, and Trollope himself at his funniest:

> The tea consumed was the very best, the coffee the very blackest, the cream the very thickest; there was dry toast and buttered toast, muffins and crumpets; hot bread and cold bread, white bread and brown bread, home-made bread and bakers' bread, wheaten bread and oaten bread; and if there be other breads than these they were there; there were eggs in napkins, and crispy bits of bacon under silver covers, and there were little fishes in a little box, and devilled kidneys frizzling on a hot-water dish; – which, by the bye, were placed closely contiguous to the plate of the worthy archdeacon himself.

Mr Harding is a mild, well-meaning man and he is particularly vulnerable to the kind of strength the Archdeacon gathers to himself through the acquisition of church patronages and bread products. Mr Harding does succeed, temporarily, in thwarting the will of his son-in-law, but despite this at the end of *The Warden* Trollope leaves his reader in little doubt about where power in Barchester really lies. Archdeacon Grantly only meets a foe worthy of his strength in the second novel in the series, *Barchester Towers*, in which we are introduced to Mrs Proudie, the wife of the new Bishop, and her oleaginous chaplain, Mr Slope.

The battles of the Proudie and Grantly factions in *Barchester Towers* take me through the spring of 2020 and into summer. Listening, rather than reading, slows down the progress of the story, so that I have no choice but to walk alongside the characters for as many hours as it takes their narrative to unfold. The recordings I have chosen of the Barchester novels are brilliantly read by Timothy West, and amongst a huge cast of characters it is possibly the determinedly low-church Mrs Proudie whom he captures most acutely. While I walk through fields of cow parsley and showers of hawthorn blossom the voices of Trollope and West take me in my imagination to Miss Thorne's fête at Ullathorne, where Mrs Proudie is in her pomp and where Eleanor Bold, now widowed, dispatches Mr Slope by boxing his ears in a secluded corner of the garden. *Barchester Towers* concludes with the Proudies still regnant at the Bishop's Palace, but with Archdeacon Grantly's chief high-church ally, Mr Arabin, ensconced both in the true seat of ecclesiastical power at the Deanery, and as Eleanor's new husband.

*

The Warden was published in 1855, following a favourable reader's report submitted to Trollope's publisher, Longmans. The anonymous reader conceded that the subject – Church corruption – was not 'very promising'. But 'such is the skill of the author that he has contrived to weave out of his materials a very interesting and amusing tale'. Trollope was sufficiently enamoured of the characters he had created to return to them in *Barchester Towers*, published in 1857, but it was not until he embarked on the fourth title in the series, *Framley Parsonage* (1861), that he began to consider the novels as a cohesive group.

The third novel, *Doctor Thorne* (1858), shares only a location and some peripheral cast members with the first two Barchester stories; *Framley Parsonage* extends the clerical circles of the Deanery of Barchester outwards into the county, taking in a new generation of clerics, gentry and aspiring politicians as it does so. By the time the young heroes and heroines of the two final novels in the series are attempting to make their way in the world, Mr Harding is an old man, Mrs Proudie's reign is coming to an end and even Archdeacon Grantly has mellowed enough to allow his son's marriage to Grace Crawley, the daughter of the impecunious and temporarily disgraced cleric whose sufferings form the substance of the final volume of the series.

The three later novels – *Framley Parsonage*, *The Small House at Allington* (1864) and *The Last Chronicle of Barset* (1867) – were all first published in serial form, which may partly explain why they suit the leisurely pace required by audiobook reading. Their plots meander, taking in sub-groups of characters who populate the offices, clubs and lodging-houses of London. These novels are also characterized by shifting preoccupations – national and clerical politics, love affairs, class differences, loneliness, family relationships and much more – and different themes and characters fade in and out of focus as Trollope's fancy dictates.

*

I resume my year in Barsetshire in the autumn of 2020, as the news fills again with rising infection numbers and the reality of a looming second lockdown. On chilly October mornings I make my way back up the hill and out of town once more, dodging puddles and ice-rink patches of fallen leaves as I go. I am now in the company of Dr Thorne and the Greshams of Greshamsbury and am following the trials and tribulations of Frank Gresham's wooing of Mary Thorne.

As the country locks down again in November, I make my way to Framley Parsonage, where I meet Mark Robarts and his sister Lucy, as well as his friend Lord Lufton and Lord Lufton's intimidating mother. There I am also reintroduced to Griselda Grantly, daughter of the Archdeacon and granddaughter of Mr Harding, a young woman so immaculately dim-witted and calculating (and voiced with such insipid venom by Timothy West) that she takes her place alongside her father as one of Trollope's most memorable creations. My autumn at Framley Parsonage also gives me my first glimpse of the seemingly omnipotent Duke of Omnium, in whose house young Mark Robarts is corrupted, and of the political machinations that fall under the Duke's control.

As autumn fades into winter, and as 2021 opens with yet another lockdown, I take refuge with Mrs Dale and her daughters at their small house at Allington, walking through the rain as the afternoon light fades in order to snatch some moments alone and outside. Trollope wrote that Lily Dale was his favourite heroine, but the moments I cherish in *The Small House at Allington* have less to do with Lily's romantic travails than with the adventures of her suitor John Eames's fellow-lodgers at Mrs Roper's London boarding-house.

The novel's masterstroke lies in the depiction of the downfall of Augustus Crosbie, who is punished for jilting Lily first by his marriage to Lady Alexandrina de Courcy and then by the activities of Alexandrina's family, who I first met at the Ullathorne festivities in *Barchester Towers*. Crosbie knows that he has been caught in a trap of his own making from the moment he is taken carpet-shopping by his prospective bride and her powerful sister Lady Amelia, and that his fate will be to be poked and nagged and worn down just like the carpet he cannot afford:

> 'That might do,' said Alexandrina, gazing upon a magnificent crimson ground through which rivers of yellow meandered, carrying with them in their streams an infinity of blue flowers

. . . Lady Amelia poked it with her parasol as though to test its durability, and whispered something about yellows showing the dirt. Crosbie took out his watch and groaned.

Alexandrina gets her carpet, along with a house in St John's Wood to put it in which Crosbie rapidly comes to hate. A kinder fate awaits Lily Dale, who remains in the small house at Allington with her mother, determined to remain her own woman in the face of her family and friends' objections.

Lily Dale keeps to that determination in *The Last Chronicle of Barset*, to which I turn as spring appears again in the Devon lanes through which I walk. The crayon rainbows have faded now, but the hedgerows are once again ablaze with colour. As the nation emerges blinking into the sunshine, unsure of its future and counting its losses, I count down the hours left before I must leave Barsetshire behind me. At the Palace the Bishop is vainly attempting to wrest control of the diocese from his wife; and in the clergyman's house at Hogglestock Mr Crawley is enmeshed in a nightmare from which there is apparently no escape. Salvation comes through the good offices of John Eames and the fortunate reappearance of Eleanor Arabin, who now only very occasionally dwells on the afternoon when, as a young widow at Ullathorne, she boxed Mr Slope's ears.

*

My year in Barsetshire has come to an end now. As I look back on the time I spent in the company of Trollope's characters I find myself wondering why they caught my attention so completely, and why the experience of hearing their stories, rather than reading them, felt both significant and right. I think it is because of the brilliance with which Trollope weaves his characters in and out of the novels, so that you truly feel you are inhabiting their world. In the gaps of time between the novels the characters age as the generations shift, but they always remain true to themselves and the stories about them already told. The result is that as a listener you feel as if you are just dropping in at the cathedral close, the Deanery and Plumstead Episcopi, or at the small house at Allington, Framley Parsonage, Greshamsbury and the clergyman's house at Hogglestock. These places and their occupants seem as real and substantial as it is possible for an imagined community to be, and the experience of listening to their stories is more akin to catching up with the news of absent friends than it is to reading a novel.

In this year of crisis the voices of Barchester have offered me the best kind of distraction. I would be desolate at losing their company were it not for the fact that I have now followed the Duke of Omnium and his young cousin Plantagenet Palliser into Trollope's parliamentary novels, and am currently listening to the intertwined stories that make up the Palliser series. I also know, from the testimony of just a few among the millions who discovered the delights of the Barchester novels long before me, that the county is not a place you visit only once. Although the circumstances will be different, I hope it won't be too long before I am able to spend a year in Barsetshire once again.

DAISY HAY's new book, *Dinner with Joseph Johnson* (2022), tells the story of the men and women who gathered around the publisher Joseph Johnson in the final decades of the eighteenth century, and of the dinner parties at which he brought them together. The cast at these dinners was extraordinary – Mary Wollstonecraft, Joseph Priestley, Henry Fuseli, William Wordsworth, Thomas Paine and William Blake were just a few of those who joined the table – but the catering was nothing like as magnificent as that on offer at Plumstead Episcopi.

The illustrations in this article are by Gwen Raverat from *The Bedside Barsetshire* (1949).

On Juniper Hill

NICOLA CHESTER

Flora Thompson's *Lark Rise* has always felt like home. A romantic notion, perhaps, from someone brought up in the 1970s and '80s, rather than a century ago, as Flora was. I first read it when I was 13, then again in my twenties, and once more recently, this time as a mother, looking back on my own childhood but also on that of my children, as the oldest two began to make their way into the world, away from the rural hamlet and tenanted ex-farmworker's cottage they've grown up in. With the passing of time that feeling of home-coming has only grown stronger.

It is, of course, very unusual that a rural, working-class woman, born the eldest of a large family in 1876 and growing up poor and largely self-educated, should have had anything published, let alone such a lyrical, yet unsentimental account of country life. But its unlikely origins make it all the more illuminating and genuine. Part lightly disguised memoir, part nature writing, *Lark Rise* is an honest, pragmatic, joyful and, at times, political record of Flora's childhood in the 1880s, and it still has resonance today.

Howard Phipps, 'A Primrose Bank', wood engraving

Though Flora, whom she calls Laura in the book, was very much of her community (the tiny hamlet of Juniper Hill, in north-east Oxfordshire), she was set apart from it too, much like the rural poet John Clare. Her father, initially a

14

stonemason, had ambitions for his craft and family and held radical socialist views in a community of farmworkers amongst whom he did not intend to remain. Their rented 'end house' had its back to the other cottages, looking outwards across the fields. But Flora's father remained a bricklayer, a 'lost and thwarted man', and the growing family stayed poor.

Formerly a rectory nursemaid, Flora's mother loved storytelling, but reading for pleasure was considered an idle indulgence, and above the station of those in the hamlet. An early and then voracious reader, Flora herself was seldom seen without a book. Though she was mocked by her peers, Flora loved to read and to wander the fields and woods alone – and that was something I identified with. At each of the five village primary schools I went to, I was accused of thinking myself 'posh' for reading. And even now, as a librarian in a rural secondary school, I find reading is viewed in much the same way by some parents, who feel their children should be helping at home, and by some children, who'd rather be out in the fields.

Flora developed a forensic, reverent and delighted naturalist's eye that she applied to both the domestic particulars of daily life – cooking, washdays and housework – and to the work that went on in the fields around the hamlet. That eye served her well as a writer. She revels in the local dialect, playing on the 'grinsard' or greensward of the grass verges and knowing all the flowers and 'craturs' living there, and while she is sometimes wistful in noting the passing of time, she is neither sentimental nor nostalgic. She records how home life, characters, entertainment and employment were all driven by the seasons and by the farming year, and she writes of pleasure, hard work, conflict and resolve.

While what Laurie Lee called 'a thousand years' of rural life was coming to an end, communities like Lark Rise were still struggling with the repercussions of enclosure, where common land (and the age-old opportunity for self-sufficiency) was fenced off and denied them. Some of the hamlet's houses, like Old Sally's, had been built 'before the open heath had been cut up into fenced fields and the newer houses had been built to accommodate the labourers who came to work in them'. Flora remembers Old Sally's fondly. Well into the next century, a whiff of any combination of drying herbs, apples, onions, malt, hops or a 'dash of soapsuds' took her straight back to her childhood. And she notes that 'Country people had not been so poor when Sally was a girl, or their prospects so hopeless.' Flora's parents, on the other hand, were the 'besieged generation . . . and the hamlet's chief assailant was Want'.

Flora does not romanticize or ennoble the poverty of Lark Rise but simply records it. 'Men afield', still hungry after a breakfast of bread and lard, might pare and gnaw a turnip pulled from the fields or 'even try a bit of the cattle's oilcake'. When I was a child, we used to pass close by Juniper Hill on our way to see my Northamptonshire nan. The daughter of an itinerant agricultural labourer, she told me how home and income could so easily be lost then. Her father was followed home one day after pulling a mangold (grown as sheep's fodder) from the ground to supplement a meagre pot at Dropshort Cottage. Confronted at the door by the farmer, her father grew angry and threw the mangold (a substantial root vegetable) at his retreating employer and landlord's head. It connected, and both cottage and job were lost in an instant (if satisfyingly so).

Flora recalls too the strength afforded by community cohesion: 'The women wished above all things to be on good terms with their neighbours.' She details a fascinating system of respectful borrowing (a spoonful of tea or the heel of a loaf to tide a household over until pay day, when it would be repaid) and the appearance of 'The Box', containing a baby's layette that was shared around after each new birth. Most families in the hamlet kept a pig, snug against their outer cottage walls, and they were generous around the time of each pig-killing. Bread was a 'heavy item' on the purse, so spilled grains of corn were 'leazed' at harvest time for flour, and the community had its 'knowledge of herbs', made jams, jellies and wine from the hedgerows, cured bacon and ham, brewed beer and grew vegetables in their small allotments and gardens.

They also knew, Flora notes, 'the now lost secret of being happy on little'. Rude health and stoicism were a source of pride, and all repeated the mantra 'I didn't flinch', whether facing a hard day's work on an empty stomach or the arrival of another baby. Along with the division of labour, the women had their tea hour and gossip, the men their pub, politics and singing. Flora records the games, gaiety and celebrations of May Day, Harvest Home and Christmas, and the last echoes of country songs, ballads and game rhymes.

The gradual creep of mechanization, industrialization, universal suffrage, compulsory schooling, better transport and communications and, eventually, the First World War, all conspired to alter country life forever, for good and bad. In Lark Rise there was both a resistance to and wariness of change (might things become worse, as they had before?) and an embracing of it, in the hope of a more comfortable life in the future. This largely self-governing community wasn't closed to the changes gathering pace outside, and this was poignantly illustrated by the women's attempts to be fashionable on slender means and cast-offs. For, as they said, 'You don't want to be poor and look poor, too.'

In 1884, 2 million agricultural labourers were given the vote and Laura observes the rise of differing politics in the hamlet. Life still felt feudal, but the desire to rent a cottage, and not be tied to one through work 'at Master's bidding', was a bid for a tenanted freedom that even now I recognize, having myself moved from tied to tenanted accommodation on big country estates.

Sympathies and intolerances swung about, before settling on a kind of acceptance with the shrugged words, 'but 'tis natur'. In a time of great social reform, some of the prejudices held by an isolated community were showing signs of shifting, though anybody living more than five miles away was still regarded as a 'furriner', and the younger married men began to share some of the home labour or ''ooman's work'. Then too, though the dreaded new school inspectors didn't hide their contempt for the 'slow wits' of country children, Flora saw their intelligence, and recorded how a new teacher 'taught them for the future, not the past . . . poor people's souls were as good, and as capable of cultivation and greatness'.

Flora began writing *Lark Rise* more than half a lifetime later and it was published in 1939, on the eve of the Second World War. It was an instant success, perhaps because it appealed to readers hankering after simpler times, when the countryside and its traditions had not yet been ravaged by change, when resilience and self-reliance brought people through hardship.

She was encouraged to write more, and two sequels, *Over to Candleford* and *Candleford Green*, followed in 1941 and 1943. They chart her move from hamlet to village to small market town, via a career as an assistant post mistress, and mirror the changes taking place in the rural working life she was leaving behind. Yet in her mind Flora never left Lark Rise entirely – and nor have I. We seem always to be walking away, distracted by the wayside flowers, but casting lingering last looks over our shoulders even as we move inexorably forwards.

NICOLA CHESTER is the granddaughter of agricultural labourers and a Romany Gypsy. She grew up in the countryside and has spent her adult life in small rural communities, living in tied and tenanted farmworkers' cottages on country estates, where the rural past never seems far away. Her memoir, *On Gallows Down*, was published in 2021.

Flora Thompson's *Lark Rise* (328pp) is now available in a limited and numbered cloth-bound edition of 2,000 copies (subscribers: UK & Eire £18, Overseas £20; non-subscribers: UK & Eire £20, Overseas £22). All prices include post and packing. Copies may be ordered by post (53 Hoxton Square, London N1 6PB), by phone (020 7033 0258) or via our website www.foxedquarterly.com. The two sequels, *Over to Candleford* and *Candleford Green*, will be reissued in one volume (400pp) as a Slightly Foxed Edition this coming June and can be pre-ordered now (prices as above).

A Glorious Menagerie

ANNE BOSTON

'Of all the civilizations of the ancient world, none enjoyed such a close and significant relationship with the animal realm as that of the ancient Egyptians.' So Philippe Germond, an Egyptologist at the University of Geneva, plunges into his subject in *An Egyptian Bestiary* (2001). But already he is outflanked on the facing page by the regal profile of a leopard's head carved in sunken relief, the sharply incised contour framing it with a powerful line of shadow. Which is fitting, for this is above all a picture book, led by 280 spectacular photographs (mostly credited to his co-author Jacques Livet) of artworks that speak across the millennia and challenge the imagination.

The book is subtitled *Animals in Life and Religion in the Land of the Pharaohs*. Gazing at the familiar, fabulous and mythical beasts haunting its pages – painted, engraved, sculpted and written as hieroglyphs – feels like falling down Alice's rabbit hole or peering through a long telescope that carries you far back in time. These beings were worshipped, feared, hunted, tamed, herded, fed, eaten and pampered by our distant ancestors when the pharaohs came to rule over the world's first nation state.

 What the text explains, the images reveal: their numinous beauty stems from the nature of the ancient Egyptians' relationship with the world around them. Unlike the cosmol-

---

Philippe Germond and Jacques Livet, *An Egyptian Bestiary: Animals in Life and Religion in the Land of the Pharaohs* (2001), is out of print but we can obtain second-hand copies.

ogy of the Bible, in the Egyptian cosmos the birds and beasts of this world and the next all find their place alongside human beings: equal if not superior in status to their human counterparts. At the dawn of the world there was no hierarchy within the universe: 'Humankind was not the final crowning achievement of creation, but was simply one of its elements, on a par with stones, plants and animals.'

I found this credo strangely comforting during the long months of lockdown, when the non-human world acquired extra significance. In the city bursts of birdsong, foxes patrolling darkened streets, seeds sprouting on windowsills were proof of the natural world's turning seasons regardless of human crisis. More crucially, clean air and clear skies brought pressing issues of climate change, pollution and destruction of wild habitats into sharper focus. All this would have been recognized by the people of ancient Egypt, who believed that the natural balance must be preserved at all costs to fend off drought, flood, famine and plague.

Ancient Egypt didn't impinge on my childhood; it wasn't even in my sights as I dawdled in a local second-hand bookshop one Sunday a couple of years ago. I was interested in the country's colonial and post-colonial history, for purely personal reasons: I wanted to learn more about Egypt at the turn of the twentieth century when my maternal grandfather, about whom I knew almost nothing, was posted to Cairo to teach in the new veterinary college. He stayed in Egypt for twenty years until his sudden death, rising to become Chief Veterinary Inspector of Lower Egypt and being awarded medals by the Khedive and the Protectorate's Sultan for his pioneering work deploying a vaccine against the cattle plague then ravaging Africa. Why did he choose to make his life in that sweltering land of river and sand so far from his native Derbyshire? Somewhere in the literature I thought I might find clues. Instead, I came face to face with a black-muzzled jackal god wearing a striped headdress, gazing out from a dustjacket. Enthralled, I paid up and struggled home with my prize – *An Egyptian Bestiary* weighs in at 2.25 kilos.

Well, here were Egypt's animals – a glorious menagerie: tangential, yet oddly familiar. As I turned the pages the dreamlike succession of images recalled that matchless passage in Penelope Lively's novel *Moon Tiger*:

> Like anyone else, I knew Egypt before ever I went there. And when I think of it now . . . I have to think of it as a continuous phenomenon, the kilted pharaonic population spilling out into the Nile valley of the twentieth century, the chariots and lotus, Horus and Ra and Isis alongside the Mameluke mosques, the babbling streets of Cairo, Nasser's High Dam . . . Past and present do not so much co-exist in the Nile valley as cease to have any meaning. What is buried under the sand is reflected above, not just in the souvenirs hawked by the descendants of the tomb robbers but in the eternal, deliberate cycle of the landscape – the sun rising from the desert of the east to sink into the desert of the west, the spring surge of the river, the regeneration of creatures – the egrets and herons and wildfowl, the beasts of burden, the enduring peasantry.

So many aspects of that ancient civilization defy comprehension today – not least the unchanging form of these artworks over the course of a mindboggling timespan. Compare the transformation in our own visual arts lexicon over the past century and a half with the formulae reproduced on the walls of sealed tombs buried under sand over 3,000 pharaonic years. For millennia, the familiar sideways profile of human face and body with forward-facing eye and torso endured, likewise the colours of sun and desert and water – ochre, sand, rust, black; turquoise, green, lapis, gold – and the mysterious imposing figures of animal- and bird-headed gods. So too did the columns of hieroglyphics, studded with owls, ibis, scarabs, snakes – of some 700 signs in the Middle Kingdom's written language, one in four use images of living creatures . . .

Another thought to try to get one's head around: ancient Egyptians had no word for art in their language. These exquisite images, created by skilled craftsmen using the finest materials, appeared only in underground tombs and those flat-roofed burial plots called *mastabas*, rarely seen by the living. Their purpose was to keep the deceased's memory alive for their survivors, and for their resurrection and eternal survival. To render a subject visually was to give it permanent existence: texts and images not only symbolized the rich life awaiting the mummified deceased but *became the things themselves* in an ideal everlasting present. Death was a rite of passage at the start of a long underground journey strewn with obstacles towards the eternal afterlife, which was, as Germond writes, 'a comforting extension of life on earth, played out in the same natural habitat populated by the same animals, and featuring the same activities, joys and woes'.

Here we are pitched into the mythical cosmos of a people living thousands of years ago, who used images to express themselves in a symbolic language that constantly shifted between the real and the imagined. A century ago, European Egyptologists confidently explained the symbols and beliefs behind the decorated tombs then being unearthed to feverish worldwide interest. Today's experts hesitate to assume anything, speculating that even the ancient Egyptians' concept of time was radically different from our own present-day historical perspective.

Germond, careful not to over-interpret, describes rather than explains, dividing his subject matter into two parts: the secular and sacred worlds. Thus arranged, the sequence of images in Part I, 'Animals in Association with Man', offers an astonishingly realistic record of the Nile region from ancient times.

The fabled 'land of papyrus' – a marshy hinterland of lakes and swamps, dangerous, mysterious yet revered as a place of birth and rebirth, 'the image of the world's very origins' – no longer exists, lost to desertification and urban development, except in the images painted and carved by the ancient Egyptians in their tombs. Early pre-Dynastic potsherds show the Nile valley rich in game – gazelle, ibex, hare; later bas-reliefs and wall paintings trace with cartoon-strip clarity farming and stockbreeding as well as hunting and fishing. We see farmers of the Old and Middle Kingdoms domesticating cattle, dogs, asses and pigs (force-fed hyenas and antelopes didn't catch on). Horses, imported from Asia in the seventeenth century BC, were not ridden but harnessed in pairs to chariots carrying driver and archer. Dogs, cats, monkeys, baboons were immortalized as faithful companions in the afterlife. (Camels and water buffalo arrived only with the Arab conquest in the seventh century AD.)

No Edenic pastoral where lion lies down with lamb, this paradise is life itself with all its dramas: a calf snatched by the cowherd from a crocodile's jaws, tongue stuck out in terror, head turned back to its fearful mother; a flurry of wildfowl flushed from a papyrus thicket in a hunt; villagers harvesting figs while baboons on the branches above plunder the fruit. The images are so vivid, so real, it's hard to hold on to the dual narrative, the funerary context: 'Ploughing and harvesting *in the afterlife*', the caption to Fig. 54 insists, and '*Symbolic* hunting expedition in the marshes' (Fig. 115).

In Part II, 'The Sacred World', the pantheon of gods and goddesses, magic, myths and legends attest to the seething world of the Egyptian imagination – the shapeshifting gods in wondrous combinations of human, animal and monstrous hybrid, balancing the sun between their ears or horns, and/or the rearing cobra, crowns of the two kingdoms and all manner of other carefully coded headgear. How to interpret scenes so resistant to definition yet so vivid, so imbued with conviction? In prehistoric times, Germond hypothesizes, Egyptians viewed animals – lion, crocodile, hippopotamus – as frightening manifestations of the uncontrollable forces governing their world. Later, in more settled times, they added human attributes to their gods but 'any tendency to favour only the human form of any given divinity, at the expense of the original animal form, would have been fundamentally at odds with the basic tenets of Egyptian thinking'. Hence the fusion of both in their pantheon, and the dual role . . . It's a theory: take it or leave it.

Sacred animals are a rich source of confusion. 'The distinction between animal god and sacred animal is not a neat and orderly one,' Germond warns. Ritual burial of individual animals had taken place from early times, as the living *ba* (essence) of a god, though this was not the same as animal worship. Greeks and Romans, whose deities (usually) took human form, were bemused by the Egyptians' veneration of animals – Greek to Egyptian in a fourth-century BC Athenian play:

> I couldn't bring myself to make an alliance with you; neither our manners nor our customs agree . . . You worship the cow, whereas I sacrifice it to the gods. You hold the eel as a great divinity, we regard it as by far the greatest delicacy . . . If you see a cat in any trouble, you cry, but I am perfectly happy to kill and skin it . . .

But Greeks after Alexander did adopt the cult of the sacred Apis bull, chosen by priests for its special markings, stabled in Memphis and buried in a huge stone coffin in Saqqara. Colossal stone statues of this figure, worshipped by Egyptians as Osiris/Apis and by Greeks and Romans in Alexandria as Serapis, testify to its awesome potency. Ptolemaic incomers also favoured the popular cat cult around Bastet, the purring homely alter ego of the fearsome lioness-headed goddess Sekhmet who symbolized the sun's merciless heat when the Nile's waters were lowest. Thousands of miniature votive statues – and once, millions of mummified cats, ibis and falcons bred and killed for the purpose – bear witness to widespread belief in objects imbued with magic; Germond concedes that by then priestly interpretations had given way to outright animal worship.

The wall paintings, reliefs and statues that appear in *An Egyptian Bestiary*'s pages were photographed on site, many in *mastabas* and tombs at Saqqara; images of amulets, scrolls and smaller treasures come from the Louvre and other European museums. Beside the magnificent photographs, the translated academic text, dense with deciphering the multi-layered imagery, assumes the reader knows more than a novice like me, while the lack of an index (regrettably normal in French publishing) and list of illustrations are drawbacks. But helpful captions interpret baffling images; and useful appendices include a chronology and an illustrated table of Principal Gods and their Animal Associations (though Osiris – *Osiris!* – is missing).

The jackal-headed being shown on the book's dustjacket is Anubis, the Embalmer. This attentive god, sometimes seen leading the deceased into the afterworld, drew me likewise into the labyrinth. I read more . . . Eventually I visited Cairo. I found no trace of my grandfather except indirectly, meeting a last peasant family farming in the built-over Delta, and visiting an equine hospital in the city. But flying in as thick brown dusk fell over the green-bordered silver Nile snaking across the sea of sand, I glimpsed what kept him there.

ANNE BOSTON's anthology *Wave Me Goodbye: Stories of the Second World War* was recently reissued as a Virago Modern Classic.

No Moral Compass

GUSTAV TEMPLE

During the first year of lockdown I decided to read the entire canon of Patricia Highsmith. I'd read *The Talented Mr Ripley*, but I wanted to see what the less famous novels were like. I would not, however, recommend this blanket immersion; at least not if you value a good night's sleep. Highsmith's books have a way of creeping up on you, especially when read sequentially, and gradually demolishing your faith in human nature.

There is no moral compass in a Highsmith novel; there isn't even a moral windsock. The reader is tossed into the Highsmith universe, where neither good nor evil necessarily triumph, where there is rarely any redemption for anyone, and the only lesson to be learned from life is that nothing is true except 'the fatigue of life and the eternal disappointment'. This line comes from the mind of David Kelsey, the protagonist of *This Sweet Sickness* (1960), Patricia Highsmith's sixth novel, and he reaches this bleak conclusion while standing on a window ledge, having got himself into a right old mess. Having read all twenty-two of Highsmith's novels, this was the one I immediately wanted to reread. Why? Perhaps it struck a chord. The premise is something everyone has experienced: the pain of chasing a former lover who has moved on. Of course, this being a Highsmith story, the doomed lover cannot simply sit around crying into his whisky and boring his friends. Oh no.

David Kelsey takes the chasing of an ex-lover to scary levels of

Patricia Highsmith, *This Sweet Sickness* (1960)
Virago · Pb · 320pp · £8.99 · ISBN 9780349006284

self-deception and what would today be categorized as stalking. Annabelle is his ex-girlfriend, now happily married to Gerald Delaney. To David's mind, however, she has sold herself short and deserves a better man, in other words David. How can he win her back and give her the life she deserves? He refers to this quest as 'The Situation' and it dominates his entire waking life (and also his dreams, which are not for the faint-hearted).

David lives a double life. He spends the week in a boarding-house in Froudsberg, a fictional small town in New York State. Every Friday, he tells the residents that he's off to spend the weekend with his sick mother in a nursing home. But he actually goes to a remote country house he's bought under the name of William Neumeister.

As soon as David arrives at his country house, he mixes two dry martinis, one for him and one for Annabelle – who is happily drinking Frascati with her husband 100 miles away. And so begins a wretched, lonely weekend, brightened only by the possibility that, when he gets back to Froudsberg on Monday, there might be a letter from Annabelle – which there usually isn't. Highsmith uses the letters between the two characters to portray their respective states of mind. Annabelle's are breezy, chatty and non-committal (and there are very few of them), while his are urgent, desperate and pleading (and there are lots of them). Hers end with things like 'This letter is so long already and I've got tons of sandwiches to make for a picnic tomorrow!' David's end with things like 'If you go, believe me that you are in my thoughts day and night and always. I will love you as long as I live.'

The appeal of this book, as with most Highsmith novels, is that the reader is given the opportunity to sympathize with the central character, though only at first. We've all, like David, projected our emotional needs on to someone who is not equipped to fulfil them for whatever reason. Some of us have also played the waiting game, hopelessly believing that the object of our desire's current relationship will fizzle out and the great reunion will take place. We may even innocently dream of the day when true love will triumph.

What most of us don't do, however, is drive to the ex-lover's house at midnight and demand to see them, pushing aside their spouse and smashing up the furniture. David's increasingly desperate measures lead him into acts that soon become criminal.

His alter ego William Neumeister is his better self, and the country house, lovingly fitted out with the finest furnishings, becomes the symbol of all that he is capable of. 'He whistled as he crossed the living room. There was something like a pleasant, huge cloud in his brain, a weightless blue-gray cloud, the colour of Annabelle's eyes. No troubles, no worries could get in. It was William Neumeister's cloud.'

As long as David, inhabiting the imaginary persona of Neumeister, floats about in his Taj Mahal of adoration, occasionally kissing photos of Annabelle placed in every room, he is safe from reality. But as soon as anyone tries to puncture the illusion, all hell breaks loose. David has a couple of friends who seem to get on his nerves even at the best of times, and the minute either of them tries to talk some sense into him, he rejects their advice:

'I said you don't want a girl you can have, you want a girl who doesn't want you. It's a neurotic symptom,' Wes said cheerfully, rocking on his heels with his hands in his pockets. 'I'm thinking of your welfare. I'm trying to give you some good advice. I don't care *who* she is.'

David's reply shows that he is already a long way from wise counsel:

'We're going to be married in a very few months, maybe less than that, and anybody who says anything different just doesn't know what he's talking about.'

Annabelle certainly thinks differently. She's just had a baby with Gerald, but even this news doesn't dampen David's resolve. He dismisses the child's existence, breezily declaring that he and Annabelle can have another one. In fact David's feelings towards her are so delusional that he shares his plans with her as if she too is desperate for them to be together. Annabelle's patience begins to wear thin and we get the impression she is only indulging David to keep him from doing anything rash (not knowing that he already has).

David reaches boiling point about a third of the way into the novel, when he tries to secure Annabelle for himself and in doing so presses William Neumeister into service. The crime he commits leads to an investigation by the police, which David handles by making phone calls to them as Neumeister, then appearing as David in face-to-face interviews. And so his double life becomes a juggling game, as he switches from one identity to the other, though unlike Jekyll and Hyde neither David nor Neumeister is the good guy.

Soon he is hopping between various locations in New York State, trying to maintain all the spinning plates he has set in motion under both identities. His mental collapse comes to a head during a startling scene at a New York restaurant where, with only $8 in his pocket, he orders an expensive meal for two, even though he is alone. To bewildered looks from the waiters, he chats to an imaginary Annabelle in the empty chair next to him:

'You're looking especially pretty tonight. Had you really rather go to a movie than go dancing somewhere?'
She demurred. She would decide after dinner. The full red skirt of her dress, crimson as fresh blood, lay on the bench seat between them and touched the dark blue material of David's trousers.

This Sweet Sickness is one of Highsmith's most accomplished works. Her own tumultuous relationships with unsuitable or unavailable women played a large part in its writing. 'Give me fantasies any day!' she once wrote in a diary. 'Fantasies of making love to an attractive friend who is unavailable . . .' During the writing of *This Sweet Sickness* she was fantasizing about an affair with Mary Ronin and by the time she had completed half the novel, the affair had become a reality. Both women were in relationships with other women at the time. Many secret meetings and passionate letters later, the affair came to an abrupt end, leaving Highsmith to travel alone to Europe, bitter and disappointed.

Many of her friends commented that, had she not found an outlet in writing, Highsmith would have ended up either in prison or in a mental institution. She wrote the sort of letters that David writes to Annabelle, often to married women. And as for the split personality, Highsmith often signed autographs in the name of Tom Ripley, the favourite of her fictional creations. She was a fan of Dostoevsky, and there are echoes of *Crime and Punishment* in *This Sweet Sickness*, as well as Patrick Hamilton's *Hangover Square*. But in both those works, one has the sense that the writer is using fiction to explore the deranged descent of a madman, whereas in Highsmith's case, it is more likely that she was exploring her own demons.

The author of this article edits *The Chap Magazine* under the name of GUSTAV TEMPLE, but that is as far as he plans to take the use of a pseudonym.

Fulmar, Gannet and Puffin

MAGGIE FERGUSSON

In shelves to the left and right of the fireplace in our dining-room, my husband keeps an extensive collection of books about Scotland. Half a shelf is given over to volumes on St Kilda. If ever I feel the need to escape from Hammersmith to a landscape of vast skies, mountainous waves, sea-spray blowing like white mares' tails across the rocks, this is where I turn: to the extraordinary archipelago, 110 miles west of the Scottish mainland, whose black cliffs and dizzying stacks, the highest in Britain, unfold in a drumroll of Gaelic names – Mullach Mor, Mullach Bi, Conachair.

Inhabited for over a thousand years, St Kilda wasn't properly mapped until 1928, and the lives of the islanders, though well documented, seem to push at the boundaries of credibility. Old sepia photographs show short, stocky men in tam-o'-shanters, dirty white woollen jerkins and plaid trousers, out of which stick bare feet with claw-like toes, formed over years of swarming up practically sheer cliffs to catch birds, which they then tucked into their belts. Despite being surrounded by the sea, the St Kildans' main diet was not fish but fulmar, gannet and puffin.

Swept by salt winds, crops were poor: there were few vegetables, and no fruit. When the first apple was brought to the islands in 1875, it caused consternation. News arrived slowly: the islanders kept praying for the good health of William IV long into the reign of Queen Victoria. If they felt the need to send letters to the mainland, the

Karin Altenberg, *Island of Wings* (2011)
Riverrun · Pb · 384pp · £9.99 · ISBN 9780857382337

St Kildans would stuff them into 'mailboats' – hollowed-out lumps of wood inscribed PLEASE OPEN – and launch them into the sea like messages in bottles. If they required more urgent attention, they lit bonfires, hoping to catch the attention of crofters 45 miles east on North Uist.

The islanders had looms, cows, sheep, dogs. Some had shoes fashioned from the carcasses of gannets. But perhaps the best way to get a feel for

Hilary Paynter, 'St Kilda', wood engraving

these cragsmen-crofters is to make a list of what they did *not* have: horses, ploughs, spades, locks, money, laws, crime.

St Kilda is top of the list of places I hope to visit before I die. So imagine my amazement when I discovered that two roads away from us in London lives a woman who has not only been there, but has also written a novel based on Hirta, the main island.

An archaeologist by training, Karin Altenberg was fed up with her job when she decided to journey to St Kilda, to blow away the cobwebs and think clearly about her future. She was to have travelled to the islands with a lobster fisherman but – as often happens – the Atlantic surges were too perilous. She caught a lift instead on a yacht. After eight hours' sailing, the cliffs of St Kilda loomed up ahead – 'like Mordor', says Karin's partner, the poet Robin Robertson. The clouds lifted and the sun came out. The combination of light and mist was, Karin says, 'otherworldly'.

No visitor is allowed to stay on St Kilda, so in the few hours she had there she rushed about taking in everything she could – the 'clachan', a huddle of oval dwellings, a bit like puffin burrows, in which the St Kildans lived until the mid-nineteenth century; the stone houses of the 'new' village; the plain, austere church built to plans drawn up by the great lighthouse builder Robert Stevenson (grandfather of Robert Louis). As she re-boarded the yacht to sail back to Scotland, an idea began to form in her mind. She would capture St Kilda not by employing her training as an archaeologist and historian, but through fiction.

Island of Wings, published in 2011, centres on a real Church of Scotland minister, Neil MacKenzie, who arrived on St Kilda in 1829 with his wife, Lizzie. The novel is, in a sense, a portrait of their marriage. MacKenzie is handsome, courteous, filled with zeal as he plans to convert the islanders from near-savages into upstanding Christians. He is fastidious – newspapers arrive months late on St Kilda, so he makes a point of reading a paper on the same date it was published, but a year on – and, when crossed, he is prone to violent rages. Though he knows he should love his flock, he is revolted by the way they live:

> The beds are dug out of the thickness of the walls, and the entrance to these grave-like beds is two by three feet. Ashes, dirty water and far worse are spread daily on the earth floor and covered every few days with more ashes. This way, they tell me, the thickness of the floor accumulates over the year so that by springtime, before this human manure is dug out and spread across the fields, the inhabitants have to crawl around their houses on their hands and knees.

Lizzie, though she arrived on St Kilda not understanding a word of the islanders' Gaelic, is less hidebound, more sympathetic: a freer spirit. In one of the most magical passages in the novel, she walks naked into the sea on a warm summer night and is illuminated by phosphorescence. Over time, it is Lizzie, not Neil, who forges friendships.

But life on St Kilda, while sometimes enchanting, can be darkly terrifying, even to Lizzie. Her first child, Nathaniel, dies in an agony of cramps and convulsions within a few days of birth. One of the island women, Betty, having lost six infants in the same way, tries – unsuccessfully – to hang herself. Betty and Lizzie draw close. Neil is fired with jealousy.

Fact is the enemy of fiction, some novelists believe. But throughout *Island of Wings* Altenberg remains true to history. Sixty per cent of babies born in St Kilda died of the 'eight-day sickness' – possibly as a result of the fulmar oil wiped on the umbilical stump after birth; possibly simply because the knives used to cut the cords were filthy. Yet though her research is impeccable, you never feel the weight of it: she has read deeply, then flown free. And throughout she evokes the islands – sometimes brooding, sometimes beautiful – with a skill that transports you.

'The archipelago', she writes, 'grew out of the low clouds like bad teeth in a weak mouth.' 'Somewhere in the west a thin band of light was breaking through the North Atlantic mist, dyeing it the colour of old sheets.' Gannets appear 'whitewashed and graceful with heads that looked as if they had been dipped in custard'. The sea mist rolls in over the island 'like the smoke of a spent battle'. In early spring, when the islanders are close to starvation, waiting for the birds to return from the west, they are pelted with hail 'as big as fulmar eggs', while sheep blow off the cliffs 'like drifting snow'.

This spellbinding imagery is all the more remarkable when you know that English is not Karin Altenberg's first language. Brought up in Sweden, where she taught herself a bit of English by reading *The Golden Treasury* and singing along to pop music, she only arrived in the UK, to take up an Erasmus scholarship, when she was 22. Perhaps it's because she has to think hard about words that she writes with such beautiful precision.

Neil MacKenzie was greatly admired by his Church of Scotland brethren on the mainland – and rightly so. Under his supervision, the St Kildans left their fetid burrows and built themselves stone crofts, with drains. In *Island of Wings*, he strips down to his shirtsleeves to join in the heavy work alongside the men. He persuaded benefactors in Scotland to donate beds, crockery, chamber pots. But this 'improvement' was double-edged. 'Faced with the prejudices of the outside world,' Altenberg writes, 'the islanders understood they were lacking in something important, something that would make them human in the eyes of the world.' Equality and co-operation, for which the St Kildans had been famed, gave way to mistrust and jealousy.

Spiritually, meanwhile, they resisted MacKenzie's teaching. 'They can repeat the catechism like a child repeats a nursery rhyme,' MacKenzie writes. 'But they do not seem to feel the weight of its truth on their souls.' Why believe in the Gospel miracles when their own pagan superstitions were so enchanting? Pluck a live puffin, the St Kildans believed, and its feathers would grow back as white as snow. His equilibrium upset by the islanders' resistance to instruction, MacKenzie suffers a mental collapse.

Island of Wings closes in May 1843, with the departure of the MacKenzies after fourteen years on St Kilda. But I can't resist fast-forwarding from this point to 29 August 1930 when, after two impossibly harsh winters, the 36 men and women still living on St Kilda were evacuated to Scotland. Many were provided with jobs working for the Forestry Commission – ironic, since they had never seen trees. They were desperately homesick, and most died before the outbreak of the Second World War, some of the common cold, which they had never before encountered. As they had prepared to depart from St Kilda, they had lit fires in their hearths, and left their bibles open at the Book of Exodus.

MAGGIE FERGUSSON is the author of *George Mackay Brown: The Life*, and Literary Editor of *The Tablet*. London-bound, she yearns to be in St Kilda. You can also hear her discussing the life and work of George Mackay Brown on our podcast, Episode 11, 'Orkney's Prospero'.

The Art of Bookselling

CHRIS SAUNDERS

Just as most good books aren't really about the things they say they are, Penelope Fitzgerald's *The Bookshop* (1978) isn't really about a bookshop. It's about English insularity, politics, the misuse of power and the headstrong persistence of hope, with Florence Green's Suffolk bookshop a symbol for every newcomer who ever found their best intentions beaten down by suspicion and hidebound tradition. At the end of the book, the formidable local matriarch Mrs Gamart manipulates her MP nephew into pushing through Parliament a bill specifically designed to close down Florence's shop in favour of a local arts centre. The arts centre is Mrs Gamart's pet project, and the town of Hardborough falls into line behind her. Florence has to conclude that 'the town in which she had lived for nearly ten years had not wanted a bookshop'. That is the last line of a book about a bookshop. An upbeat ending it is not.

As someone who runs an antiquarian bookshop, Henry Sotheran Ltd in London, I feel all this in a very raw part of my soul. However, I don't think Fitzgerald is really writing about the bookshop industry. Indeed, the resistance Florence meets to her new shop is something that most of us would find unfamiliar. In my home town of Battle, which is not entirely dissimilar to Fitzgerald's fictional Hardborough, our excellent new local bookshop Rother Books was welcomed with open arms three years ago and continues to thrive. It's clear that Fitzgerald is using the bookshop to explore the innate conservatism

Penelope Fitzgerald, *The Bookshop* (1978)
Flamingo · Pb · 176pp · £8.99 · ISBN 9780006543541

of the English, which is really encapsulated in the furore caused when Florence decides to stock the recently published *Lolita*. Mr Brundish, Florence's most influential supporter, puts his finger on the issue:

'It is a good book, and therefore you should try to sell it to the inhabitants of Hardborough. They won't understand it, but that is all to the good. Understanding makes the mind lazy.'

Lazy is comfortable, though, and the bookshop makes some people very uncomfortable indeed. *Lolita* is the rallying point for Mrs Gamart's campaign against Florence's shop, ironically because of its popularity. The 'undesirable attention' caused by the window display of the 'unduly sensational novel by V. Nabokov' brings enough disruption to the High Street to allow Mrs Gamart to lodge a formal complaint with Florence's solicitor. Florence's refusal to apologize and withdraw her bestseller from sale stiffens the matriarch's resolve and bolsters her case against the shop as a public nuisance.

This is the sort of perception that can only come from someone who has actually worked in a bookshop. You soon learn that some of your customers are very conservative, and that some subjects will always sell. Fitzgerald notes that certain customers will buy anything by anyone who has been in the SAS and also by 'Allied commanders who poured scorn on the SAS men'. That holds true to this day, and I love these people, for their dedication pays the bills. She also pinpoints the conservatism of the market in the distinction between books that are 'stickers' and those that are 'stayers'. Stickers are terribly hard to sell, and include philosophy and poetry. Stayers, such as reference books and dictionaries, are the books you always keep in stock because, although unexciting, they fulfil people's needs. Stickers and stayers go to the back of the shop. The window is reserved for the 'aristocratic' – in Florence's case, 'luxurious' books about country houses that, like their owners, demand their place at the front by 'right of birth'. It is funny that, for Fitzgerald, the English class system applies even to its books.

There are always exceptions to these rules though. Every now and again, the bookshop owner encounters a collector with interesting taste, an enquiring mind and a deep pocket, and the meeting of minds is invigorating for both parties. Florence has just one such customer, Mr Brundish, whose introductory letter describes a passionate engagement between customer and bookseller from a lost golden age of bibliophilia:

> In my great-grandfather's time there was a bookseller in the High Street who, I believe, knocked down one of the customers with a folio when he grew too quarrelsome. There had been some delay in the arrival of the latest instalment of a new novel – I think, *Dombey and Son*. From that day to this, no one has been courageous enough to sell books in Hardborough.

Supporters like Mr Brundish bring real hope to the bookseller. During hard times such as we have experienced recently, they can be the difference between survival and the unthinkable opposite. All things must pass, though, and when Mr Brundish, the only person with more influence in Hardborough than Mrs Gamart, dies, Florence's bookshop is doomed. It is a lesson to all booksellers – cherish your best customers but never forget to cultivate more.

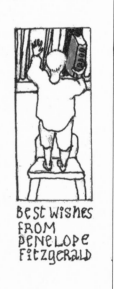

Best Wishes from Penelope Fitzgerald

You also have to know your market. Nothing is worse for business than selling books that aren't quite right for the customer. Florence's bookkeeper is unnerved to see the number of 'returns inwards' caused by buyers not liking their books and returning them: 'They're shocked, or say they've detected a distinct tinge of socialism.' The balance between pushing exciting literature and not frightening the horses is something no bookseller has ever entirely mastered.

This problem is central to the buying of stock, which is a complicated art of selection, negotiation and guesswork. Florence, as a seller of new books, deals with publishers' reps, while as an antiquarian dealer I tend to deal with individuals with books to sell, but the basic process described is the same. Things have changed nowadays for new booksellers, but in the 1950s the reps would slog through the countryside to visit your shop with a selection of stock and would negotiate better prices on popular books as long as you took some of their less exciting wares:

> Those [reps] who made [the journey] were somewhat unwilling to part with their Fragrant Moments and engagement books, which were what Florence really wanted, unless she would also take a pile of novels which had the air, in their slightly worn jackets, of women on whom no one had ever made a demand.

There is also the logistical problem of transporting and storing large loads of books. Winding Suffolk roads make life difficult for Florence; the Byzantine puzzle of the central London one-way system does the same for us. Then there is the awful intuition that unsold stock is just dead weight, summed up when, after the compulsory purchase of the shop, Florence discovers there would be 'no claim for depreciation, as books were legally counted as ironmongery'.

All these pressures mean that, like many other bookshops, including ours, Florence's premises find themselves being used by people for secondary purposes that sound like a good idea at the time – people such as Theodore Gill, a persistent and prolific local water-colour painter, who arrives 'smiling as a toad does' with bundles of dreadful paintings that he expects Florence to exhibit. She is finally able to fob him off, despite him hanging small paintings willy-nilly on her shelves, but she does succumb to the idea of running a private circulating library. This is hugely time-consuming, highly unprofitable and ultimately disastrous when Mrs Gamart imperiously picks up books reserved for other customers and causes an actual riot. The financial pressure on bookshops to diversify and provide other services – coffee, cake, juggling workshops – is still very real and demands a whole range of skills that the dedicated bookseller might not have or, indeed, be interested in acquiring. A bookseller simply wants to sell books to like-minded people, and Fitzgerald understands that perfectly.

I have always thought that, although this novel is about more than just a bookshop, it must have been written by someone with insider knowledge. It was no surprise to learn that in the 1950s, when Penelope and her husband Desmond were hard up, she took a part-time job at the Sole Bay Bookshop in Southwold, run by the very genteel Phyllis Neame. In her 2013 biography of Fitzgerald, Hermione Lee reports Fitzgerald's rather nostalgic feelings about her time there:

Mrs Neame . . . would have been horrified at the idea of on-line bookselling, and so would the customers, who thought of the shop as the one place to go on a wet day (and the weather can be very bad in Southwold). They would hang about for hours and go away without buying anything – except perhaps one greeting card – but we never complained, that would have been against the tradition of bookshop keeping.

Like Florence's shop (and, we think, Sotheran's), the Sole Bay Bookshop had a poltergeist. Penelope and Phyllis had a long debate about stocking *Lolita* and, in the end, went ahead. The dreaded novel didn't bring Phyllis's bookshop down, which at least paints a rosier picture of English tastes than Fitzgerald's book, but Phyllis was reportedly quite upset by the depiction of Southwold as Hardborough, insisting it was all much nicer, as I'm sure it was. *The Bookshop* isn't a *roman-à-clef*. It's a funny book, but it's also so gloomy in its conclusions that it does make you fear for the future of British culture.

From my own place in the book industry, I really don't think it's as bad as all that. We have a lovely clientele who buy books across all kinds of subjects and who love a good chat about whatever they're reading, and we all learn from each other. Yet any bookseller will recognize the world Fitzgerald creates, and she is absolutely right in pointing out that you should never, ever employ an 11-year-old girl with a Donald Duck ruler to run your private circulating library.

CHRIS SAUNDERS is the managing director of Henry Sotheran Ltd, the country's oldest antiquarian bookseller. He is also a writer on bookish matters and runs the literary blog Speaks Volumes. You can hear him discussing the world of antiquarian and second-hand bookselling in our podcast, Episode 12, 'Slightly Foxed – But Still Desirable'.

Not So Verray Parfit

SUE GAISFORD

I once taught English at a girls' school in which the head of department didn't like poetry. It's an odd aversion but it worked well for me. The poetry room was right at the top of a very tall building, and thither wended her way every pupil in the place, to be rewarded by peaceful sessions chewing over every kind of poem, from epic to lyric to limerick. But some of these girls also had to pass public exams. The A-level syllabus was dictated by a higher authority and this term the poetry module featured Chaucer. No problem in that. To me, he is the tops. He understood the complicated, subtle, self-deluded and some-times glorious nature of human beings better than any writer, before or since, and he displayed enough humour, generosity and lightly worn erudition to keep a whole pilgrimage entertained from here to eternity.

The story selected from *The Canterbury Tales* was, however, 'The Knight's Tale'. It is the only really tricky one. The language is quite easy, but the story itself makes your heart sink. Set in vaguely classical times, it is very long and, despite being extremely bloodthirsty, profoundly boring: enough to put these students off the great man for life. Based very loosely on Boccaccio's *Teseida*, it tells the story of Palamon and Arcite, knights and cousins who fall in love, almost simultaneously, with the lovely Emelye, sister-in-law of Theseus. There follows a great deal of extremely violent fighting until Arcite is

---

Geoffrey Chaucer's *The Canterbury Tales* (1387–1400) is available in a Penguin paperback (528pp · £7.99 · ISBN 9780140424386). Terry Jones's *Chaucer's Knight: The Portrait of a Medieval Mercenary* (1980) is out of print but we can obtain second-hand copies.

killed and a tetchy Theseus orders Emelye to marry Palamon and be done with it. There is precious little to endear the reader to any of these characters, and to call it a Romance seems absurd.

How, why, could Chaucer have written such tedious stuff? Virtually every other pilgrim is described with wit and irony aplenty, yet the only academic studies available to a teacher insisted that the Knight was genuinely the epitome of virtue and his wretched story a marvellously heroic and chivalric tale. There was no option but to set about it with as much enthusiasm as possible.

And then, as if by magic, the postman delivered a new book, sent from the *Economist* for urgent review: *Chaucer's Knight* (1980) by Terry Jones. It was an exciting moment. For a start, the author was one of the Monty Python team, which boded well; then just a quick look at his Preface showed that this was probably going to be the answer to a maiden's prayer. 'I could not understand', he wrote (obviously having read my mind), 'why such a man could have written such apparently dull pieces as "The Knight's Tale", "The Monk's Tale" and "The Tale of Melibee".' His book, most comprehensively, enjoyably and convincingly, sets about giving the answer.

It begins with the Knight's description in the Prologue, which is heavy on battles. Previous scholars had, for centuries, blithely assumed that all these were heroic endeavours, crusades undertaken to spread Christianity into a heathen – or, more accurately, an Islamic – world. Not a bit of it. The very first mentioned, for example, the siege of Alexandria, was notorious for the appalling behaviour of the Christian knights. Alexandria was a rich and thriving port, peacefully inhabited by many different races, and an important centre of the spice trade. When, on the morning of 10 October 1365, the large fleet gathered by Peter of Cyprus arrived in the old harbour, the citizens flocked cheerfully down to meet the ships, ready to do business.

The resultant massacre spared nobody, male or female, young or old, Muslim, Jew or even Christian. The city was comprehensively sacked, its churches, synagogues and mosques looted, thousands of its inhabitants slaughtered and 500 people enslaved. After three days the 'crusaders' departed with their booty, leaving the ruins to fall back into the hands of the infidel. As the Benedictine historian Thomas Walsingham observed not long after the event, the only tangible result was that the price of imported spices shot up.

By Chaucer's time, anyway, the very notion of crusading had become tarnished. What did so much bloodshed have to do with promoting a religion of love and peace? It would be hard to make a case for there being any evangelizing benefit at all in such forays. The Knight claimed to have 'reysed' (or raided) in Lithuania more often than any other Christian of his rank. After those raids the score, according to that same Walsingham, was 4,000 slain or captured as against eight converted: not much of a return. And so it goes on. Every one of the battles listed in the Prologue would have been notorious to Chaucer's first audience, who would at once have realized that this knight was not what he pretended to be.

The Great Schism, which began in 1378, produced two, later three Popes, all at war with each other, and all scandalously employing soldiers of fortune, Christian against Christian. It is easy to imagine the reaction of Chaucer's early audiences when they heard the knight apparently praised for riding to war 'as wel in cristendom as in hethenesse'.

I'd studied medieval history for A level but had never thought of putting Chaucer so firmly in his historical context. How blinkered we were. Of course we should have questioned what a proper, noble, 'parfit' knight was doing fighting all these foreign wars when he was so clearly needed at home. England was having a dreadful time after the appalling loss of life in the Black Death. The Peasants' Revolt and the many subsequent uprisings terrified people. 'Although I may weep over it,' wrote Chaucer's friend John Gower, 'I shall write of a tearful time, so that it may go down as an example for posterity . . . my heart and hand tremble.' The war with France had led to frequent raids all along the south coast, as well as such great epic battles as Crécy and Poitiers. These, and the recurrent threats from Scotland, required every able-bodied knight of the realm to defend king and country. And all the while Chaucer's gallant knight was busy fighting for anyone who would pay him, far from home.

This scruffy knight, accompanied by a 'yeoman' armed to the teeth (a longbow in the 1380s was a battlefield weapon), wore no identifiable heraldic device, no coat-of-arms, nothing at all to allow him to be recognized, no insignia of the chivalry he professed to admire. This was actually illegal, but it made for a quick getaway if things got too hot for him.

In case any doubt remained as to his probity, more evidence keeps on coming. As a diplomat, Chaucer had been to Milan in 1378 to suggest a marriage between Richard II and Caterina, daughter of Bernabó Visconti, the terrifying 'tyrant of Lombardy' (as well that the match never happened). At the same time, he met Sir John Hawkwood, leader of the notoriously powerful and savage White Company of mercenaries, who was married to another Visconti daughter and who, Jones points out, had many grim characteristics in common with our scurrilous knight. There is a clue to this in the near-contemporary Ellesmere manuscript illustrations of the pilgrims, where the knight's war-horse is branded with an M, which could well be code for Milan. And in his tale, the statue of Mars is adorned with the revolting symbol of a wolf devouring a man, directly identifying it, to its early audiences, with the hated and feared Visconti.

This is just one of the many ways in which the elegant graciousness of Boccaccio's *Teseida* is vulgarized and distorted by its pretentious and unconvincing narrator. Another example is the Temple of Venus. In Boccaccio, the temple contains a garden of delights, writes Jones, where 'Comeliness, Elegance, Affability and Courtesy walk arm in arm'. Chaucer's knight finds only 'debauchery, expenses, lying, flattery and even force. Instead of birds of every kind, sparrows and doves, he sees only the cuckoo sitting on the hand of Jealousy, in itself a parody of the courtly hawking image.' The fact that so few, if any, scholars seem previously to have made such detailed comparisons might be due to the fact that the *Teseida* was not even translated into English until 1974. Gradually unpicking all the clues is serious, scholarly, painstaking and analytical detective work, but it makes genuinely thrilling reading.

I reviewed Jones's book accordingly but was then faced with a further problem. What to tell my students? There was no middle way. Either this fellow was a glorious soldier, with a story to tell of love and honour – or he was a ridiculous fraud. I wrote to Terry Jones, asking him how his book had been received by the kind of academics who might be marking A-level papers. He replied saying that the only bad review had been written by a woman whom (he was ashamed to say) he had not treated well when they had both been undergraduates – and, incidentally, could he come and talk to our girls about it all?

On the appointed afternoon, the lower floors of the school emptied upwards as everyone crowded into the little poetry room. All the staff were there, even the unpoetic head of English and the netball teacher, and Terry Jones did not disappoint us. He started by asking what we thought of knights, showing us a Breughel painting of armoured horsemen apparently handing out presents to villagers.

The next picture, of an X-ray of that painting, showed the real horrors of the original. It was *The Massacre of the Innocents*, and the parcels became babies, snatched from their mothers or impaled on swords. Perhaps, he suggested, knights weren't always gallant, romantic and brave after all?

He told us that he'd begun really thinking about this book while filming *The Life of Brian* in North Africa. He'd asked a local historian whether he knew anything about the English soldiers who had been in that part of the world during the fourteenth century. The answer succinctly confirmed a suspicion he'd been harbouring. 'They were the very worst and most feared of all the mercenaries.' Jones spoke for two hours, never pausing. Nobody wanted it to end: we were, en masse, enraptured.

Gradually, school life resumed its humdrum normality and, as the glory of this most excellent of lecturers faded, my girls settled down to revision. By then, they had been thoroughly seduced by the Terry Jones approach, so I suggested that – if they chose to use it – they should also point out, for their own security, that many fine and respected scholars ignored it, preferring the traditional interpretation . . .

. . . and, astonishingly, with a very few honourable exceptions, they still do. Fellow Python Michael Palin, lamenting this fact, says that it is because people like to pigeon-hole each other: 'If you're a comic, then that's the box you belong in, and there you should stay,' although he has himself largely escaped such a straitjacket. Whatever the reason, nearly all academics, study guides and commentaries still carry on in the tedious and unconvincing old ways, as if this remarkable book had never been written. The great, clever, generous Terry Jones died just as this article was being written. It might be timely for them to have another think.

SUE GAISFORD is a freelance journalist, which isn't quite the same thing as a mercenary. She has been a literary editor, interviewer, columnist and critic, and now mostly reviews books.

Fresh as Paint

ARIANE BANKES

My brother, my sister and I grew up in a rambling farmhouse in Hampshire hung with pictures by friends of our parents, for they knew a wide range of artists and tended, naturally, to buy works by people they knew.

Some of these paintings seemed gloomy and frankly baffling, but those by Julian Trevelyan and his wife Mary Fedden danced with life and colour. Julian and Mary were among our favourite week-end guests, and we were particularly in thrall to Julian, who loomed over us from his immense height with his 'craggy welcoming face and patriarchal beard', in the words of his cousin Raleigh Trevelyan. He would spend hours entertaining us with comic drawings, notably of himself as Edward Lear's 'old man with a beard/ Who said "It is just as I feared!/ Two Owls and a Hen/ Four Larks and a Wren/ Have all made their nests in my beard."'

We looked forward, too, to their Christmas cards, etched by Julian and usually featuring their cats; in our dog-only household these  alluring felines insinuated their way into our imaginations and took firm hold. I was to meet those cats and their successors when I moved to London in my twenties and took to visiting the Trevelyans in their studio at Durham Wharf in Hammersmith, two boathouses that

---

Julian Trevelyan, *Indigo Days* (1957), is out of print but we can try to obtain second-hand copies.

seemed to float above the shifting tides of the Thames, interconnected by a luxuriant small garden.

The wonderful living-room with its broad window giving on to the ever-changing Thames waterscape is memorably described by Julian in his memoir *Indigo Days* (1957):

> The walls, beams and ceiling we painted white, and we were enchanted with the ever-changing patterns of the reflections from the water on the ceiling whenever the sun shone. At times the sailing boats seemed almost to sail into the room and the gulls to swoop around the beams.

He captured this watery quality in a numinous painting of 1946, *Interior, Hammersmith*, which was exhibited in Paris and admired by Georges Braque, who subsequently invited Julian to tea to encourage his ambitions as a painter.

Julian writes of stumbling upon the property in 1935 with his first wife, the potter Ursula Darwin: newly married, they were searching for a home where Ursula could erect her kiln on a plot of land or a derelict wharf, when they passed a 'To Let' sign outside a couple of dilapidated sheds on the river, the former studio and home of the sculptor Eric Kennington. 'The tide was up and gulls flew screaming round us while tugs and sailing dinghies slapped about in the choppy water; we realized instinctively that this was our home and that we could live nowhere else.'

Though primarily an artist, both painter and experimental print-maker (he taught at Chelsea School of Art and the Royal College of Art, where he became Head of Printmaking), Trevelyan had a flair for writing, and was the author of essays on a wide variety of subjects, as well as several books about the artist's life and calling, of which *Indigo Days* is the most personal and seductive. It covers the first half of his long and eventful life, three decades during which he developed his unique artistic personality and vision. This was distilled out of the bohemian, gregarious years he spent in Paris, London and the industrial north, during which he immersed himself by turns in surrealism, abstraction, landscape painting, satire and social comment. Add in his extensive wartime travels and his love of the exotic, and you have a boldly imaginative and original take on the world.

The only surviving son of R. C. 'Bob' Trevelyan, a classicist and minor poet, and 'a charming eccentric, at once childish, passionate, foolish and wise', Julian inherited many of his father's characteristics, notably his sociable nature. Bob Trevelyan's circle of friends extended to Bloomsbury and beyond, Roger Fry, Bernard Berenson and Bertrand Russell prominent among them. Regular expeditions from their home in Surrey to the Trevelyan family seat, Wallington, in Northumberland, took the impressionable young Julian rumbling north by train through the gritty industrial heartland of Britain, instilling in him a lifelong love of factories, 'vast railway stations, and valleys full of smoking chimneys'.

Going up to Cambridge in 1929 to read English, he found it dominated by a generation of poets, and fell in with the likes of William Empson, 'who rolled his great eyes round and round as he read his poems', Malcolm Lowry, Julian Bell, who would tragically be killed in the Spanish Civil War, Kathleen Raine, 'slight and beautiful as a flower', and Humphrey Jennings, who kept Julian up to the mark with the admonishment, 'That picture of yours hasn't got 1931ness.' It was Jennings who opened his eyes to contemporary French art. Paris seemed to be the epicentre of all that was exciting, so Julian abandoned his studies, packed his bags and moved to Montparnasse.

There, he found himself among 'a sort of international riff-raff of writers, painters, tarts and scroungers, all speaking together in bad French, [who] floated through the cafés, peering amongst the sea of tables on the pavements for a friend or acquaintance'. When not attending painting classes, or prowling round unknown corners of the city, he would frequent the legendary Café du Dôme – 'the hub of the world, the cauldron in which all the races on this planet were being cooked into one gigantic *bouillabaisse*'.

His neighbour was the American sculptor Alexander Calder, who was then developing his mechanized circus of wire acrobats, sword swallowers, tightrope walkers and chariots, which he would set to performing on a green baize circle in his studio. More often than not they came to grief, for 'the frailty of his mechanisms was part of their charm. Over his bed were a series of strings that put on the light, turned on the bath, lit the gas under the kettle and so forth; often they failed to function and he would have to hop out of bed to fix them. When I last saw him,' Julian writes, 'he told me he was making a machine for tickling his wife Louisa in the next room.'

He also met the painter and engraver Stanley William Hayter, owner of the legendary studio Atelier 17. Here, he presided over a laboratory of printmaking by artists as various as Joan Miró, Alberto Giacometti, André Masson and occasionally Pablo Picasso – who was reputed to have *flambéed* his lunchtime steaks on the etching plates. The possibilities of this form of image-making fascinated Trevelyan, setting him on a course of experimentation that would make him one of the notable printmakers and teachers of his day. And the work of his surrealist contemporaries inspired a series of dream-like images that would culminate in his magical 'Dream Cities' of the mid-1930s. Ever interested in the workings of the subconscious, he later volunteered for experiments with the hallucinogenic drug mescaline, under the influence of which, he wrote, he had 'fallen in love with a sausage roll and a piece of crumpled newspaper from out of the pig-bucket'.

Back in London, the raging Spanish Civil War diverted his attention to politics, and thence to the experimental Mass Observation movement, dreamed up by the anthropologist Tom Harrisson to record the habits and concerns of the English, just as he had studied the peoples of Polynesia. The northern town of Bolton became the anonymous 'Worktown' and its pubs, shops and dance halls the sites of research. As designated artist for the project Trevelyan found himself trundling around with 'a large suitcase full of copies of newspapers, copies of *Picture Post*, seed catalogues, old bills, coloured papers and other scraps', applying the collage techniques he had learned from the surrealists to his depiction of that Depression-era industrial world. From Bolton they travelled to Northumberland to meet the Ashington miners, or 'Pitman Painters' as they are now known, whose talents and intellectual curiosity profoundly impressed Julian; a lively debate on the motion 'That anyone can paint' and a touring exhibition of their work followed.

Then came war, and conscription to a camouflage unit, where he and the theatre designer Oliver Messel were initially charged with disguising pillboxes newly erected against the German threat.

> We camouflage officers were given full rein to our wildest fancies . . . and to this day, I believe, there exists [a pillbox] on the pier of St Ives that I had turned into an old Cornish cottage with cement-washed roof and lace curtains. Elsewhere I had erected garages complete with petrol pumps, public lavatories, cafés, chicken-houses and romantic ruins.

Camouflage techniques took him on zany expeditions across Africa and the Middle East, where the tones and textures of the jungle, the desert, Cairo, Alexandria, Jerusalem and Lagos answered his appetite for the strange and exotic. When asked by his commanding officer to identify his religion at this time he defiantly wrote 'Surrealist'.

This is a painter's memoir, informal, intimate, steeped in colour, vivid, deeply serious yet often comic in detail – and fresh as paint, still, after all these years.

ARIANE BANKES co-curated the exhibition *Julian Trevelyan: The Artist and His World* at Pallant House Gallery, Chichester (October 2018 – February 2019), and still loves the nonsense verse of Edward Lear.

Hammering Away at Words

ANDREW NIXON

'Why do I feel as if the Earth is disappearing from under my feet?' was the reaction of one friend when I introduced him to Hooting Yard, the 'nonsense' literary universe created by that most cultish of cult writers, Frank Key. Yes, you must have a care when approaching Hooting Yard. Make sure you're sitting down or at least have something solid to grab on to, because vertigo is guaranteed as you are struck by a series of dizzying revelations.

It starts with the sheer scale of the thing. In 2007 the *Guardian* said of Frank Key that 'he can probably lay claim to having written more nonsense than any man living', and in the subsequent years until his untimely death in 2019 he wrote a lot more still. Key's oeuvre consists of millions of words, mostly arranged in short, sharp stories set in Hooting Yard, a warped interpretation of England. The stories are collected in fat paperback anthologies with titles like *Impugned by a Peasant* and *Unspeakable Desolation Pouring Down from the Stars*. Hundreds of the tales can also be read in the online library hootingyard.org, or heard declaimed in the author's gluey East London growl as podcasts – the legacy of Key's long-running weekly radio show for Resonance FM.

So, where to set sail on this ocean of words? It actually doesn't

---

Mr Key's Shorter Potted Brief, Brief Lives (2015) is available from Constable in hardback at £12.99. Frank Key's anthologies *Impugned by a Peasant* and *Unspeakable Desolation Pouring Down from the Stars* are available in paperback from Lulu, and *By Aerostat to Hooting Yard* (2014) is available as a Kindle book. For more stories by Frank Key visit the online library www.hootingyard.org.

much matter. Pick a story at random and dive in . . . And now the next revelation will hit you, which is how *funny* Frank Key is. This is the opening to a story called 'I Had a Hammer':

I had a hammer. I hammered in the morning. I hammered in the evening all over this land. I hammered out danger. I hammered out a warning. I hammered out love between my brothers and my sisters all over this land. They should have seen that coming. As I said, before I hammered the love out of them, I hammered out a warning. It was hardly my fault if they thought I was just larking about.

It goes on from there, the narrator finally hammering away across many lands 'like an angel of death'. Humour, of course, is subjective, but Key is a master of every conceivable type of comedy so whatever the angle of your funny bone he will find a way to tickle it. He does gags, punchlines, observational wit, comic-book violence, surprise twists, startling call-backs, Pythonesque surrealism, vicious satire and the bleakest of black comedy, and he's certainly not above deploying a silly name. Hooting Yard is populated by a glorious cast of recurring characters, including intrepid explorer Tiny Enid, useless master criminal Blodgett, pathetic poet Dennis Beerpint and – most beloved by fans – Dobson, a prolific author of pamphlets on wildly eclectic topics (potato clocks, the bee as a moral exemplar, the actress Tuesday Weld . . .), all of which are always out of print. (The one that got my friend was a throwaway mention of Dobson's 114th pamphlet, 'The Mythical Island Where Werewolves Think They Come From (out of print)'. The notion that werewolves might have their own, erroneous origin myth brought on the aforementioned vertigo.)

Key can give you a sudden guffaw with a one-liner or, over the course of a story, gradually turn you into a giggling wreck by piling on ever greater absurdities – particularly when performing his own work. I have witnessed him onstage (spindly, scruffy white beard, eyes twinkling behind thick specs) reduce an audience of sixth-formers to tears of mirth with a deadpan reading of the story 'Little Dagobert' – an increasingly hilarious tale of mock-Dickensian woe and a real crowd-pleaser that begins 'I banged my head on the baptismal font, but that was only the beginning of my troubles.'

But now we come to the next thing about Key, and the principal reason for his continued status as a 'cult' rather than a bestselling comic fantasy author in the mode of Douglas Adams or Terry Pratchett. Twenty minutes after having them roaring with laughter, he had beaten that sixth-form audience into baffled silence with a lecture so arcane and incomprehensible that he might as well have been speaking Aramaic. For pleasing crowds, it soon becomes clear, is very far from the top of his agenda: indeed, there is really only one reader Frank Key is concerned with pleasing, and that is Frank Key himself. And what he likes is hammering away at words, words, words . . .

*

Paul Byrne was born in Barking in 1959. His father was a communist Labour councillor and his mother a Flemish-speaking Belgian. His early influences were socialism, Roman Catholicism and *The Beano*. As a teenager he drew cartoons and attempted without much success to sell photocopied comic strips via adverts in Terry Jones's *Vole* magazine. At the University of East Anglia he found like-minded creative types keen to publish – and in the true spirit of the punk years they did it all themselves: writing, illustrating, printing and distributing their own collections of student prose and poetry.

At this point Byrne was more cartoonist and artist than author – he sold his own strange, collaged postcards on a market stall in Norwich – but gradually the words took over. He borrowed the nom de plume 'Frank Key' from an advert for a Nottingham builders' merchant and stuck with it for the next four decades, as he ploughed his idiosyncratic literary furrow through the small-press publishing world of the 1980s and '90s (often making illicit use of the photocopier at the Islington Council office, where he worked as a welfare officer) and steadily gained a following.

Then came the Noughties and the online worlds of blogging and digital radio. It is impossible to overstate the transformational impact of the Internet on peculiar, non-commercial writers like Frank Key. The Hooting Yard style changed hardly at all between 1989 and 2019 but the Internet's cost-free global reach meant that his audience, while remaining distinctly cultish, could grow exponentially: he could even scratch a living of sorts from subscriptions and sales of self-published paperbacks.

Every now and then Key would be 'discovered' by a mainstream journalist, who would send back a missive in much the same fevered tone as a Victorian explorer announcing the unearthing of a Lost City of Gold. The *Guardian* hailed Key as the 'finest living practitioner' of nonsense fiction. The BBC's Will Gompertz effused about the 'magical world' he'd stumbled upon. One reviewer, taken aback by the depth of erudition and observational wit in Key's stories, said: 'He seems to have the whole world in his head, plus another one of his own making.'

All of Key's fans – including several commercial publishers – agreed that by rights he should have been much richer and more famous than he was. For here was a ferociously intelligent author with a total command of the English language, who seemingly could have made a lucrative living by writing anything he chose in the mainstream: criticism, journalism, novels . . . It's just that he chose not to.

*

The 'story' Key used to bludgeon that sixth-form audience into a stupor was entitled 'How to Think of Things Other than Juggling'. Deliberately employing tedium as a literary technique, it consists of a set of instructions for building an unfeasibly complex machine

('Attaching clamps to slats with quarter-inch gulliver bolts, smear some lattice-work with a decoction of binding-agents and thread the netting through tin clips . . .') and it goes on for a *very* long time, the gag being that at the end of the process you will have achieved your goal of forgetting all about juggling.

Why did Key put his audience through this ordeal-by-verbiage? Because he delighted in the crackle and crunch and weirdness of words like 'gulliver' or 'decoction' and was not much concerned about whether the sum of those words made much sense to his readers. This is the essence of Key's brand of 'nonsense': not coining words *à la* Lewis Carroll or Edward Lear (no slithy toves or runcible spoons), but rather carefully selecting real words and seeing how far he can push their meanings before they snap.

In some Hooting Yard stories the word-gaming is obvious. A number are written in a sort of plonking prose-poetry, with each sentence rhyming but not scanning. 'The Cruel Sea' is simply a list of hundreds of three-word sentences comprising the definite article and an improbable combination of adjective and noun ('The cruel sea. The dismal pond. The glued vicar. The obsolete pudding . . .'). But even in the more conventional-seeming tales, such as one of Tiny Enid's intrepid adventures, Key's narratives are continually hijacked by his own vocabulary. A striking word or pun or idiom will suddenly take him off on a completely different tack and often he won't even attempt to get back. Stories become shaggy-dog stories within even shaggier, doggier stories; gardens of endlessly forking paths; labyrinths without centres; seas of red herrings.

The same applies to the wider world of Hooting Yard. Unlike other fictional universes such as Middle Earth or Gormenghast, neither the chronology nor the geography of Hooting Yard make even internal sense. In some stories Dobson is a Victorian, in others he has use of the Internet. Hooting Yard has its places – Pang Hill, Bodger's Spinney, the Blister Lane Bypass – but it cannot be mapped for the same reason that the not-thinking-about-juggling machine cannot be built: it's all just funny words. Everything is subservient to the language. Key quite often explicitly signals his word-obsessions ('There are twenty-four points of interest between the aerodrome and the zoo, and I wish I could say they were arranged alphabetically. In a better-ordered kingdom, they would be.') and thereby gives away the impossibility of creating either an atlas or a history of Hooting Yard, though that hasn't stopped some fans from trying.

Hooting Yard is more akin to the cartoon worlds of *The Simpsons* or *Peanuts* or Key's beloved childhood *Beano* than to, say, Narnia. Characters never develop or remember anything from previous stories, but simply 'reset' with each new appearance. Real people, historical events and current affairs randomly intrude (for some reason JFK's assassination pops up all the time), because Hooting Yard is the prism through which Key can view, control and hilariously satirize reality, just like in a long-running comic strip. Frank Key was a cartoonist who came to prefer words to drawings – and that, essentially, is his unique gift to the world: a vast, wonderfully complex comic-book universe, but made of language rather than pictures.

*

In the years before the digital world changed everything for him, Paul Byrne had a difficult time. The 1990s – he called them his wilderness years – were marked by severe alcoholism, divorce and ill-health. The Internet saved him. He found readers, advocates and, most importantly, a lifelong inamorata, muse and kindred spirit who goes by the splendid moniker of Pansy Cradledew.

Paul followed a strict daily routine: rising early, working all morning, reading all afternoon. He typed out his stories using the hunt-and-peck method, one sentence at a time, testing each line by reading it aloud to Pansy before moving on to the next. He did his daily blogs and his weekly radio show and sold his books to the fans who relished his every carefully chosen word. And late in his life one of those fans – a publishing agent – even managed to find a way to

Frank Key at the Mudchute Omphalos, London, photograph by Stephanie Thomson

get him into commercial print without compromising his principles. *Mr Key's Shorter Potted Brief, Brief Lives* (2015) is an 'updated version of John Aubrey's *Brief Lives* consisting of a single, unadorned fact about each of my subjects' – the fruit of Paul's favourite hobby of squirrelling himself away in the British Library and wallowing in arcane trivia. So for his last two decades, Paul earned just enough money from his writing to live precisely as he wanted to live.

Paul died at the age of 60 in 2019, from complications of diabetes. But the vast, vertiginous literary universe of Frank Key, the 'man who can claim to have written more nonsense than anyone', will live forever on the Internet. Hooting Yard is a fathomless ocean of wonderful words, ready to welcome anyone who wants to dive in.

ANDREW NIXON is a writer from Bristol and the founder of *The Dabbler* online magazine, to which Frank Key contributed a weekly column between 2010 and 2016, never missing an instalment.

A Classical Mosaic

DAISY DUNN

Alexias was an unwanted child. When he was born, a month premature, his father took one look at his small, fragile frame and decided that he was the product of an inauspicious age and that it would be kinder to all concerned if he were killed at once. Preparations were being made to abandon him to the elements when, quite unexpectedly, news came of another death in the family.

In 430 BC, the second year of the Peloponnesian War between Athens and Sparta, the plague had begun to sweep Athens 'like fire in old heather'. Several months on, it showed no sign of abating. Alexias' grandfather had succumbed, and now his uncle, just 23 years old, lay lifeless on the floor. He had gone to visit his lover and had found him on the verge of death in the fountain where he had been bathing to relieve his fever. Bereft, and convinced that he, too, was stricken, the uncle took hemlock. As he lay dying, he traced in wine with his finger the name of his beloved: PHILON.

The Last of the Wine (1956) is the most affecting and profound of Mary Renault's historical novels. I first read it when I was taking a course in Greek vase painting as a student at Oxford, where Eileen Mary Challans (as Renault was off the page) had studied in the mid-1920s. I was struck by how sensitively she wrote about love between men at a time when homosexuality was seldom discussed. I couldn't help feeling that Renault, herself a lesbian, empathized most with those Greeks who were forced into marriage against the pull of their own hearts.

Mary Renault, *The Last of the Wine* (1956)
Virago · Pb · 416pp · £8.99 · ISBN 9781844089611

At the time I was researching a beautiful terracotta cup, made about seventy years before the Peloponnesian War erupted. It had at its centre a painting of Achilles bandaging the arm of his comrade Patroclus, both characters familiar from Homer's *Iliad*. As I looked at the details in the paintwork – the flash of white as Patroclus bares his teeth, the tension in his foot as he struggles to hold still – I had the distinct impression that Mary Renault had been here before me. The image, you see, recurs in her novel, only in a slightly altered form. Alexias, granted life after his mother dies from complications of labour, grows up and falls in love with a slightly older youth named Lysis. When Alexias cuts his foot, Lysis cleans the wound in the sea and then offers to carry him over the sand. Alexias, who narrates the story, savours the moment:

> I leaned back for him to take hold of me, and fastened my arms round his neck. But he did not carry me; nor did I let him go.

Echoing Achilles in the painting, Lysis eventually kneels down to tend to the cut, even pressing his lips against it to stem the bleeding. Alexias recovers. Like the classical vase painter, Renault clearly saw Achilles and Patroclus as more than just friends, despite Homer never having made a relationship between them explicit. She was equally inspired by reports that Socrates, a minor character in her novel, came to the aid of the Greek general Alcibiades when he was injured in the Peloponnesian War and that the two men were lovers.

This rich and rather complex layering of ideas was characteristic of Renault, who was never so heavy-handed as to allude to every painting and poem and history book she used within her narrative. She made a mosaic of little bits from here, little bits from there, and held them together with an invisible grout. Classicists love her books because they recognize the sources from which she has taken her material and they take pleasure in unpicking how she used them. But while they may know the history of the Peloponnesian War inside out from Thucydides, who charted the decline of Athens over the course of the thirty-year conflict, the human cost of that war is better understood through fiction.

Renault does not spare her readers the mess and bloodiness of war. She describes sinews tearing, bones grating, last breaths whistling in the throats of the dying. Most poignantly of all she describes the effects these sounds have upon those left standing. Alexias is violently sick when he slays a man. He is, as Renault often reminds us, little more than a teenager. As he leaves for battle, he bids farewell to his new stepmother, just eight years his senior, and catches sight of the soldier he is to become:

There was a silver mirror on the wall behind her; as I moved, I saw a man reflected in it. I turned round startled, to see what man had come into the women's rooms. Then I saw that the man was I.

His stepmother's reaction to his joining the campaign is somewhat different. 'Oh, no,' she says before he can correct her, 'you are still a boy.'

In ancient Greece, affairs between young men – and older men and boys – were deemed beneficial for emotional and intellectual development. The city-state of Thebes even had an elite infantry section formed of 150 pairs of male lovers known as the Sacred Band. The idea that an older man could inure a younger man to the realities of war through love as well as through experience appealed to Renault, who depicted Lysis as a mentor as much as a partner. *The Last of the Wine* is, at heart, a coming-of-age story in which Alexias learns to leave behind his difficult childhood and become a better man than his father.

Alexias' family live in the Inner Kerameikos, a suburb of Athens popular with potters, in a house with a courtyard, a fig tree and a colonnade of painted columns, and they own at least two horses – a sign that they are fairly well-to-do. Life should be idyllic. And yet Alexias grows up with a brute, who has him raised by his concubine, a woman so cruel that she wrings the neck of his kitten. Only the arrival of Arete, the stepmother, offers Alexias some reprieve. By contrast, the war, despite its horror, offers an opportunity to escape.

I have been reading Mary Renault again recently while writing a book on Oxford between the wars. Sitting down with *The Last of the Wine* and a couple of Renault's other novels set in ancient Greece – *The King Must Die* (1958), on the feats of the hero Theseus, and *Fire from Heaven* (1969), on the young Alexander the Great – I was again enchanted by the poise of Renault's prose and the emotional depth of her characters. Alexias, especially, emerges as only too human, riven by jealousy when Lysis reveals that he has met a girl, and by disgust at his suggestion that he, too, might like to get an early taste of what marriage is like:

> The truth was that his encouragement had rather missed its mark, reminding me that it would be he, in the natural course of things, who would get married first. People I knew seemed to take this lightly enough; I had seen them acting groomsman to their friends with perfect cheerfulness; it distressed me to think myself more given to extremes, and less capable of reason, than other men. Indeed, when I look back, I cannot understand myself at this time of my life.

Defying what remained 'the natural course of things' in the 1930s, Mary Renault found a life partner in Julie Mullard while training to be a nurse at Oxford's Radcliffe Infirmary. Her first few books were written between nursing shifts. In 1948, the two women moved to South Africa, where they found a new freedom. It was, as Alexias might have said, like fleeing the flames for a life of thrilling uncertainty.

DAISY DUNN is the author of five classical books and has made a foray into the twentieth century with her sixth, *Not Far from Brideshead: Oxford between the Wars*, published this March. You can hear her discussing the literature of the ancient Greeks and Romans in our podcast, Episode 28, 'An Odyssey through the Classics'.

Following the Music

SUZI FEAY

As deputy literary editor of the *Independent on Sunday* in the mid-1990s, it was my job to organize and compile several of the routine book columns and features every week. One such was the long-running 'The Book that Changed Me'. It involved typing up a short telephone interview with a literary or other type of celebrity; less frequently, the contributor would write the copy themselves. It can be difficult to drum up fresh ideas once a column has been underway for some time, but we never ran short of suggestions and contributions. One highlight for me was hearing Christopher Lee declaim at length down the line in Elvish, in his fanatical enthusiasm for *The Lord of the Rings*. I can only imagine how delighted he must have been to be offered the part of Saruman.

This little feature was more profound than it might have looked at first glance; it wasn't merely 'my favourite book' but the rather more exacting 'the book that changed me'. Some ideas were turned down as not quite fulfilling the brief. As with most newspaper features, the piece was usually 'pegged' to a timely event or release. The cellist Julian Lloyd Webber must have had a forthcoming album to promote when his publicist contacted me with a pitch.

What surprised me about Lloyd Webber's choice was that I had never heard of the author, let alone the book – Arthur Machen's *The Hill of Dreams*. His impassioned manner during the interview impressed me. Although I no longer remember in detail what was

---

Arthur Machen, *The Hill of Dreams* (1907)
Parthian · Pb · 200pp · £9.99 · ISBN 9781906998332

said, this mysterious novel, first published in 1907, immediately became a book I wanted to get my hands on. But, appropriately as it turned out for such a mystical writer, it proved difficult to track down.

Machen's work should really be discovered after a vigorous quest, rather than at the click of a button. The search should involve much scanning of dusty shelves in out-of-the-way bookshops in quiet towns. One such establishment, on its last legs, yielded a signed copy, numbered 22, of Machen's *The Shining Pyramid* (Martin Secker, 1925, 42s). The elderly, bearded bookseller let me have it for a tenner on account of the wormholes. (Bookshop and proprietor had both utterly vanished on a subsequent visit, which seemed somehow very appropriate.)

Other volumes of Machen began to accumulate on my shelves, as well as associated material: the graphic novelist Alan Moore is a fan, featuring Machen extensively in his book *A Disease of Language* (2005). I even went on a Machen-themed walk one Sunday, starting at the British Museum and led by a man whose gleaming eyes and long pointed fingernails were equally disconcerting. *The Three Impostors* of 1895 had been republished by Oxford Classics. A novella, *The Great God Pan* (1894), had come out with a small press. But of *The Hill of Dreams* I found no trace, until a battered 1970s paperback was eventually run to ground in an occult bookshop in Bloomsbury. The price reflected the book's rarity rather than its condition.

Once devoured, that paperback was eventually launched back into the sea of the second-hand, to find a new Machen enthusiast. My current copy is the handsome 2006 hardback edition from Tartarus Press, in which luxuriously thick pages add bulk to a fairly slender text: seven dense and luscious chapters detailing the rapturous boy-hood and despondent manhood of one Lucian Taylor, like Machen himself the son of a Welsh clergyman. Mark Valentine's perceptive introduction remarks on the 'sense of some secret reality behind the outward form of the world' which 'Arthur Machen strove . . . to communicate in all his work, especially in this, his finest book'.

Born in 1863, Machen grew up in Caerleon and went to London in his teens to scrape a living on the fringes of the book trade, and his experiences of poverty fed directly into the analogous story of Lucian Taylor. Machen had begun this visionary work a decade before publication, while living in Verulam Buildings in Gray's Inn, where friends included M. P. Shiel, the writer of macabre tales, and A. E. Waite, of Rider-Waite tarot deck fame. For a masterpiece, its passage into print was surprisingly rocky. Repeated rejections, even accusations of madness, ensued before the world was ready for Lucian's story.

The opening chapters deal with the young Lucian's rapturous explorations of the hills and vales around Caermaen (the fictionalized Caerleon) with its deserted Roman fort. 'He liked history, but he loved to meditate on a land laid waste, Britain deserted by the legions, the rare pavements riven by frost, Celtic magic still brooding on the wild hills and in the black depths of the forests, the rosy marbles stained with rain, and the walls growing grey.' It is a lonely adolescence, with the scholarly yet academically unsuccessful boy alienated from his peers. The adjective 'healthy' is used of the local bully with some scorn.

The cataclysmic central experience of Lucian's life takes place in the deserted Roman fort. Exhausted by the climb up to it, he flops to the ground, 'indulging a virgin mind in its wanderings'. His clothes seem to fall off of their own accord; he cannot see his hands. The reverie intensifies, 'the gleaming bodily vision of a strayed faun. Quick flames now quivered in the substance of his nerves, secrets of life passed trembling through his brain, unknown desires stung him.' He awakes nearly an hour later, in confusion, 'as with electric heat, sudden remembrance possessed him. A flaming blush shone red on his cheeks, and glowed and thrilled through his limbs.' Profoundly shaken, Lucian makes his way back home, determined to capture the visionary experience in words. His path – to become a writer – seems clear.

Yet the path is filled with obstacles. His father's social status as vicar has been eroded by his unorthodox views. The smug pettiness of the locals revolts Lucian, with very few kindly souls willing to give the boy a chance. He gradually learns to abstract himself from society, but his calm contemplation of the torture of a helpless puppy by the 'healthy' lad makes for the novel's most horrible scene. Machen's presentation of Lucian is ambivalent, never moralistic, as befits a work of the decadent fin-de-siècle. (Machen had been a casual acquaintance of Oscar Wilde.) On the other hand, Lucian's bitterly funny denunciations of successful contemporary fiction have the ring of being Machen's own.

The Hill of Dreams owes a clear debt to J. K. Huysmans's 1884 novel *À rebours*, whose protagonist, Des Esseintes, withdraws from a surly, uncouth world into a private haven of aesthetic delights. Lacking Des Esseintes's fortune, Lucian finds refuge only in his imagination, choosing to live, not in present-day Caermaen, but in the town as it was at the time of the Romans. In visions, he drinks the ancient vintage, sees the torchbearers, hears 'the crash of cymbals, the calling of the flutes, and the surge of the wind in the great dark wood'. Hence the significance of Machen for occultists, for whom to imagine is to experience and become.

Transposed to London in one of Machen's skilful time-shifts, Lucian tries desperately to fix his visions on the page in a drab west London bedsitter. The portrait of a part of town now gentrified (Machen lived in Notting Hill) but then still surrounded by remnants of farmland is fascinating. As earlier he tramped the Welsh hills, now Lucian wanders the streets, high on hunger and self-righteousness. The broken trees, smouldering brick-kilns and encroaching villas, row upon identical row, fill him with horror. In another great set-piece he wanders at night among shops lit by gas-jets and naphtha lamps, aghast at the cackling and howling of the populace: drunken women and men, discordant music and crazed dancing. 'He was oppressed by the grim conceit that he himself still slept within the matted thicket, imprisoned by the green bastions of the Roman fort. He had never come out, but a changeling had gone down the hill, and now stirred about the earth.'

Julian Lloyd Webber contended that *The Hill of Dreams* is dear to musicians for being the closest words can come to having the effect of music. Certainly it's not a book you read for the plot. It's a verbal symphony evoking dream states and ever-changing moods, from light and playful to blank and despairing. Though there are passages of sharp realism, it leaves the reader with impressions rather than characters or incidents (the puppy excepted). Its most dramatic events occur on the astral plane rather than in the everyday. Lucian's great love affair with local girl Annie seemingly takes place entirely in his own head, the farmer's daughter becoming Astarte, Venus, even such sinister avatars of womanhood as Salome. As a portrait of intense loneliness and isolation, the novel could not be more timely.

Machen leaves us one last ambiguity to ponder: just how good a writer is Lucian? Is his plight due to the habitual contempt of mediocrity for genius, or is he merely a hyper-sensitive who lacks the talent to express his insights? Linger in these pages and you too may find yourself tormented by the clashing of cymbals and the eerie piping of flutes.

As literary editor of the *Independent on Sunday* for eleven years, SUZI FEAY amassed a houseful of volumes, but she still can't resist the lure of a second-hand bookshop.

The Sins of the Father

HELEN MACEWAN

A. A. Milne's son musing with mixed feelings on his childhood as 'Christopher Robin'; Daphne du Maurier's daughter recalling life at Menabilly, the model for *Rebecca*'s Manderley . . . I've always been drawn to memoirs by the children of famous writers. They may not be as stirring as the life stories of the writers themselves, the Trollopes and Dickenses who emerge triumphant from youthful adversity, but those whose lives are lived in the shadow of celebrated parents have struggles and sufferings of their own. It can be as much a burden as an honour to bear a well-known name, and I'm intrigued to find out how they carry it.

That burden may be all the heavier when the parent is unconventional, a transgressor. So when, years ago, I came across a memoir called *Son of Oscar Wilde*, of course I had to read it. Written by Wilde's younger son Vyvyan, it describes the aftermath of Wilde's fall from grace for Vyvyan, his brother Cyril and their mother Constance.

The sadness of their story made a deep impression on me then. Recently I revisited it after reading Richard Ellmann's biography of Wilde and Franny Moyle's of Constance, who spent the last three years of her life in exile with the two boys following Wilde's imprisonment (she died at the age of 39 after a botched operation). Neither biography gives much more than glimpses of the two children, and Cyril, the elder son and favourite child of both parents, is more visible than his brother. Vyvyan was something of a disappointment

Vyvyan Holland, *Son of Oscar Wilde* (1954), is out of print but we can obtain second-hand copies.

from the start, since they had wanted a girl. He was thought to be delicate, an excuse to bundle him off for months at a time to friends' country houses away from the London smog. Thus, he led a peripatetic existence even before his exile.

Vyvyan

He tells us that he wrote down his story to convey 'the loneliness of being Oscar Wilde's son' and 'the cruelty of the self-righteous who believe that "the sins of the fathers shall be visited upon the children"'. The book was published in 1954; homosexual acts were not decriminalized in Britain until 1967, the year of Vyvyan's death, and he does not refer to his father's crime by name or comment much on the rights and wrongs of the case. His purpose was to describe its consequences for 'those who, although innocent, suffered in a hurt, uncomprehending way, wondering why they were not treated like other people'.

Unlike most 'son of . . .' memoirs, his tells of the anguish of *not* being able to identify himself as his father's son. When Wilde was convicted of gross indecency in 1895 Vyvyan and Cyril were dispatched with a hastily hired French governess to a Swiss hotel, where Constance joined them. They never saw their father again. It was the start not just of a period of foreign exile but of a childhood and youth of 'concealment and repression'; they returned to England three years later, following Constance's death, under a different identity. Wilde was still living at the time, but his wife's family gave them to understand that he was dead.

In the early days in Chelsea, although Wilde had often been an absent father, he was an affectionate one. The boys took into exile happy, innocent memories of playtime with him in the Tite Street nursery. Heedless of his immaculate attire, he would crawl on the floor with them. He bought them a toy horse and milk-cart and wasn't satisfied until he had filled the tiny churns with real milk, and Nanny found the three of them hurtling their cart round the room as milk slopped over the floor. These recollections in the book's first chapter establish Vyvyan as a good storyteller and someone who, like his father, can step easily into a child's world. *Son of Oscar Wilde*, related as simply as if he were telling it to his own son, is packed with vivid details.

On rereading the book I found I had forgotten just how gripping it is. I'm hooked from the moment the two boys board the train to Dover in the company of the supremely unsympathetic French governess. Every detail of the Channel crossing (spent by Vyvyan in the boat's engine-room), the railway journeys, the stuffy Parisian hotel room where, hungry and bored, they are left to their own devices on their first day of exile, is seen through the eyes of the two unhappy little boys. There is entertainment along the way, as when Constance arrives at the Swiss hotel to find that the (soon-to-be-dismissed) governess has run up a ruinous bill for candles, needed for her devotions – she has spent her time praying for her charges instead of looking after them.

Driven from the hotel when their identity is revealed, the trio move on to Italy and Germany where the brothers, often left to roam wild, prove resourceful at supplementing their pocket money, undercutting local flower-sellers in an Italian fishing village and offering themselves as guides to English tourists in Heidelberg. The educational regime changes as often as the landscape. One moment Vyvyan is enduring bullying and canings at an English school in Heidelberg, the next he is admitted to the dimly lit corridors of the Collegio della Visitazione in Monaco, run by Italian Jesuits.

'A haunted creature chased from pillar to post', as he describes himself, fear of discovery an ever-present sword of Damocles, Vyvyan spent his childhood in a state of perplexity. He didn't discover the nature of his father's offence until he was 18, imagining him variously as a burglar or a bigamist. After the scandal broke, a wall of secrecy was built to shut out all knowledge of the man he remembered as a 'smiling giant'.

'My wife sends me photographs of the boys – such lovely little fellows in Eton collars,' Wilde wrote to his friend Robert Ross from France following his release. The photos were taken in Heidelberg when Vyvyan was 7 and Cyril 9. The pair gaze at us out of the pages of the book, two solemn little boys. Wilde longed to see them but Constance was loath to allow this when he resumed his friendship with Bosie, and whatever hope he had of contact with them ended with her death.

Constance's family determinedly severed all links with Wilde. At an uncle's house in Switzerland, the boys were informed that their surname was to be officially changed to 'Holland' and instructed to practise their new signatures. New name tapes were sewn into their clothes, but at school in Heidelberg they found the old ones still in place on their cricket flannels; minutes before the first game of the term Cyril was frantically hacking them off.

Back in England after Constance's death, under the strait-laced tutelage of their great-aunt Mary, Vyvyan came across a copy of *The Happy Prince*, a book he recalled from the old days, and wondered why Wilde's name had been scratched off the cover. When he returned home for the school holidays wearing a black armband, having been told of Wilde's death by the Jesuits at Stonyhurst College

Oscar Wilde in Naples, after his release from prison

(for his classmates he invented a yarn about an explorer father, dead after a long absence), 'I had not been at my aunt's house for more than four minutes when my armband was ripped away, and it was once more impressed upon me that my life was not like that of other boys and I could not go into mourning for my father.'

We feel the pain all the more keenly because the emotion is so restrained. Vyvyan's most desolate moments speak for themselves. At 15, home for the Christmas holidays, he was turned away from the house of cousins with whom he was to spend the day, their parents having taken offence at something he had heard and repeated in all innocence, unaware of a slightly indecent double meaning. The lesson learned, as so often before, was that as the son of Oscar Wilde he was different, a pariah. Reluctant to return to his great-aunt's house after this contretemps, he was found hours later lying in the snow in a nearby wood in an attempt to freeze to death, which resulted in mastoiditis and the loss of his hearing in one ear.

All this is told without self-pity or bitterness. Rather, it was Cyril, considered the braver and stronger of the two, who became embittered. But then his burden was harder to bear; he had found out the truth about his father at the age of 10 and had had to keep it from his brother. Vyvyan tells us that the elder brother became grave and taciturn, desperate to prove himself 'a *man*' and wipe the stain from the family name. 'For that I have laboured; for that I have toiled . . . It was this Purpose which whispered in my ear,' he wrote in a letter to Vyvyan. I feel great sadness for Cyril even if his letter-writing style makes me thankful he's not the narrator of the boys' story. His chance to redeem the family honour came with the First World War; he was killed in France in 1915 by a German sniper.

As for Vyvyan, the family's solution to the problem of what to do with him was to pack him off into a second exile – in the Far Eastern Consular Service. But a few months from his twenty-first birthday, as he was listlessly cramming in dingy lodgings for a civil service exam, the wall of shame and secrecy finally began to crumble. It had started to wobble some years earlier, when a broad-minded aunt by marriage had told him the reason for Wilde's disgrace and said she found all the secrecy 'absurd'. And at Cambridge, where he was riveted by *The Ballad of Reading Gaol* after spotting it on a friend's bookshelf, he had disclosed his real identity to a few choice companions and found that they weren't shocked either. Now, through a fellow student at his London crammer, he finally met his father's friend and literary executor Robert Ross. Within months, many friends of his father's had become friends of his. For the first time he was hearing Wilde spoken of with admiration and affection.

Vyvyan barely touches on his later life in this memoir – how he escaped banishment to the Far East and instead became a translator, how he was a loving father to a son of his own. But one of my last glimpses of him reassures me he's going to be all right. Robert Ross, playing fairy godmother, organized a party for his twenty-first birthday, and we see him coming of age surrounded by well-wishers, people who honour his father's memory. As the book closes I seem to feel the lightening of a load on my own shoulders. At last Vyvyan is learning a different kind of lesson about what it means to be the son of Oscar Wilde.

HELEN MACEWAN is a translator. She is also the author of books about Charlotte Brontë's time in Brussels, which has been her home since 2004, and of a life of Winifred Gérin, a Brontë biographer with a Belgian link.

Writing under Occupation

TIM PEARS

Many writers reported finding it hard to focus during the Covid lockdowns, beset as they were by anxiety and feelings of futility. Eighty years ago, a writer produced remarkable novels under a far more onerous lockdown during the Second World War. Where we hid from an invisible virus, he was under German occupation, and then Allied bombardment.

Born in 1892, Ivo Andrić was a Yugoslav writer, and also a diplomat whose career reached its peak with unfortunate timing in 1939, when he was appointed as Yugoslavia's Minister Plenipotentiary and Envoy Extraordinary to Berlin. In September of that year German forces invaded Poland, and Britain and France declared war. Thereafter, Yugoslavia attempted a tortuous neutrality, though under increasing pressure from Germany to side with the Axis. Seeing where this pressure would lead, Andrić submitted his resignation to the authorities in Belgrade: 'I request that I be relieved of these duties, and recalled from my current post as soon as possible.'

His request was denied. Eventually, on 25 March 1941, the Yugoslav government followed Hungary, Romania and Bulgaria into the embrace of the Axis. The Yugoslav military, however, proudly refused to accept this acquiescence: two days later army officers staged a coup d'état and asserted their country's independence. Hitler was infuriated that this small Balkan country had dared to defy him. 'The hammer must fall on Yugoslavia without mercy,' he decreed. The

Ivo Andrić, *Bosnian Chronicle* (1945)
Apollo · Pb · 432pp · £10 · ISBN 9781784971120

country was attacked from all sides, on land and from the air. This Blitzkrieg lasted just ten days: the Royal Yugoslav Army capitulated on 17 April.

Ivo Andrić and the rest of the Yugoslav Legation staff in Berlin had been put on a train out of Germany. Most took refuge in neutral Switzerland, but Andrić continued his journey to Belgrade. An old friend, the lawyer Brana Milenković, met Ivo at the railway station and took him back to the house in the centre of Belgrade where he lived with his mother and sister, who made two rooms available to their guest.

As well as being occupied by the Germans, Yugoslavia was then consumed by a ferocious civil war between the Fascist Ustasha in Croatia, the Royalist Serb Chetniks and Tito's Communist Partisans. Belgrade, half ruined by the German bombardment, was now flooded with refugees. From his rooms, Andrić could see floating in the Sava river the corpses of Serbs killed by Ustasha and 'posted' to Belgrade. The bodies sometimes clogged the river under the new bridge that the Germans were building. Their engineers used hand grenades to clear the human blockage.

Reprisals for resistance to the occupiers were brutal: for any German soldier wounded, fifty Yugoslav civilians were rounded up and executed; a German soldier killed meant a hundred civilians executed. In addition, the Quisling government ordered prominent public figures to sign a proclamation that condemned all resistance. Many did sign, regardless of their patriotic feelings or political convictions. When a courier brought the text of the proclamation to Andrić for his signature, he refused, saying: 'Tell them that he wasn't at home.'

The courier, however, recognized the writer. 'But Mr Andrić,' he insisted, 'it is you!'

'Well, if you are so smart,' Andrić replied, 'you can tell them I told you that I wasn't at home,' and closed the door.

Now aged 48, Andrić retired from the Diplomatic Service but

refused to accept a pension, instead living simply on his savings. In the ruins of Belgrade, he busied himself running errands for those who needed help distributing what food and medicine could be found, and keeping spirits up. Each evening he shared the Milenković' meagre dinner. He also started writing.

Bosnian Chronicle (1945) had first been conceived almost twenty years earlier, when Andrić was a junior attaché in Yugoslavia's consulate in Paris. He made no friends there and found himself isolated and

lonely. 'Apart from official contacts,' he wrote in a letter home, 'I have no company whatsoever.' Instead, through 1927 and 1928 he spent all his free time in the Paris archives, poring over the three volumes of reports sent to the French Foreign Ministry at the beginning of the nineteenth century by Pierre David, their consul in Bosnia, and making notes. Now, in German-occupied Belgrade in 1941, armed with these notes, Andrić set to work on his novel.

Napoleon's military successes had established the 'Illyrian Provinces' in Dalmatia. The French then requested from the Ottoman Empire a consulate in Travnik, administrative capital of the Ottoman province of Bosnia, to establish safe and reliable trade routes through the Balkans. Bosnia was ruled by a Vizier, or governor, an Ottoman who found himself miserably far from Istanbul, amongst people who resented him as the representative of their oppressive Turkish colonizer.

Jean Daville, Andrić's French consul, is the principal character in *Bosnian Chronicle*, which follows him from his arrival in Travnik in 1807 to his departure – and the closure of the consulates – seven years later. Though it is apparent to the reader that the Frenchman carries out his diplomatic obligations with good grace, he is psychologically ill-suited to the role, being privately indecisive and continually tortured by the fear of having made the wrong move or misread someone else's. He, the Vizier and the Austrian consul Josef von Mitterer are engaged in a never-ending game of saying – through interpreters – one thing while meaning another, each trying desperately to decipher the truth behind his counterpart's obfuscations, and to further his own Empire's interests.

A major theme of the novel is the impossibility of communication, between east and west no less than between individuals, which is nowhere clearer than when the Vizier invites the consuls to the palace to celebrate his latest skirmish against Serb rebels. War trophies are scattered on the rug for the foreigners to admire: amid the captured weapons, Daville is horrified to realize that there are also piles of noses and ears, presented triumphantly by the Vizier, who is oblivious to the Frenchman's horror – which he in turn, for the sake of diplomacy, must conceal.

In this he is helped by von Mitterer, for the Austrian is a military man, more easily able to control his emotions. The two foreigners are bound together. 'Their unhappy fate and the difficulties it brought drove them towards each other,' Andrić writes. 'And if ever there existed in the world two men who could have understood, sympathized with and even helped one another, it was these two consuls who spent all their energy, their days and often their nights putting obstacles in each other's way and making each other's life as troublesome as possible.'

Momentous events like Napoleon's doomed assault on Moscow or the War of the Sixth Coalition take place far away. The Vizier and the consuls are puppets on a string, with fixed roles to play but powerless to influence events. They and their respective families and entourages are exiles, in Travnik temporarily, while the minor characters who people the novel, the indigenous Bosnian Muslims, Catholics, Serbian Orthodox Christians, Jews and Gypsies, watch from the sidelines.

Andrić's style is discursive. He builds a galaxy of characters, the stars and their satellites spinning around each other, their stories told in anecdotal chapters: one is devoted to the three town drunks, another to a Catholic monk dedicated to healing with herbal medicines, a third to the impossible love affair between von Mitterer's wife and Daville's young assistant. In one chapter we meet the chief member of the Vizier's household. His treasurer, Baki,

> had been keeping the Vizier's accounts for years now, conscientiously and accurately, saving every last grosch with the tenacity of an inveterate miser and defending it from everyone, including the Vizier himself . . . He ate little and drank only water, and every mouthful he saved was sweeter than any he ate.

Andrić gives us the world of Travnik in all its variety and depth, and he uses the ebb and flow of politics almost as a pretext to delve into the minds of those entrapped in the town. *Bosnian Chronicle* is at once satirical and psychoanalytical, and in both its structure and its humour, it bears striking similarities to *Catch-22*. Indeed one could hardly believe Joseph Heller hadn't read it if it wasn't for the fact that the first translation into English didn't come out until the same year as *Catch-22* was published.

The novel opens with local Muslim beys sullenly anticipating the imminent arrival of the consuls, and it ends with them enjoying the foreigners' departure.

*

Conditions in Belgrade, meanwhile, deteriorated further in 1942. Coal was rarely available, food increasingly scarce, people scavenged for scraps. Where we under lockdown suffered brief shortages of toilet paper and pasta, in German-occupied Europe people ate boiled rat-meat and pine-needle stew. That winter, thousands starved in Belgrade.

Andrić's long-time confidante, Vera Stojić, visited him regularly and typed up the pages of the manuscript of *Bosnian Chronicle* as he produced them. Then the Serbian Literary Association asked Andrić for a submission. The letter of invitation displayed the signature of a poet and translator of Shakespeare with well-known German sympathies and some influence with the occupying authorities.

Andrić replied. Instead of offering vague excuses or false promises, he wrote that he did not intend to publish anything with his country under occupation, 'while the people are suffering and dying'. He then packed a small suitcase and awaited the arrival of the Gestapo.

They never came.

After the war, the secretary who worked for the Association, and who knew Andrić's earlier work, revealed that she had opened and read the letter, and had quickly buried it in the archives before anyone else had an opportunity to see it.

No sooner had he finished *Bosnian Chronicle* than Andrić promptly started work on what would become another masterpiece, the second of his three great novels, and his most famous book, *The Bridge on the Drina*.

In 1944, from April to September, it was the Allies' turn to pulverize Belgrade. Andrić would later tell a friend, Zuko Dzumhur, how frightened he was by the sudden scream of the sirens that warned of the first raid. He ran out of the house and joined the column of frantic people fleeing the city. As he was swept along, he looked around him and realized that all these people were trying to save their families, their children, their infirm parents.

'I looked myself up and down,' he said, 'and saw that I was saving only myself and my overcoat.'

Ashamed, he turned round and went back to his rooms. Subsequently, even during the fiercest bombing, he never left the house again.

In September, fighting came to the city. 'All the windows are wide open,' he wrote in his diary. 'Rifle fire fills every day. One goes into rooms on all fours like a bandit. There is only dry food to eat. There is little water and it must be saved, as must candles, as neither the water supply nor the power station is working.'

Liberation finally arrived in October 1944: the Red Army and the

Partisans entered Belgrade, and Tito was installed as the head of a Communist-controlled government.

In March 1945 *The Bridge on the Drina* was the first book published by Prosveta, the newly founded Serbian state publishing house. Successive editions sold out. *Bosnian Chronicle* followed later that year.

In October 1961, Ivo Andrić was awarded the Nobel Prize for Literature. That he wrote two of his three great novels (the third being *Omer Pasha Latas: Marshal to the Sultan*) in such desperate conditions makes his accomplishment all the more extraordinary, and inspiring.

TIM PEARS is the author of eleven novels, most recently the *West Country Trilogy* (2017–19) and the collection *Chemistry and Other Stories* (2021). He is very grateful to Celia Hawkesworth, Biljana Djordjević Mironja and Zoran Milutinović for their kind help with information for this essay.

You can hear Tim Pears talking about his own novels on our podcast, Episode 19, 'Tim Pears's West Country'.

A Fresh Take on the '45

URSULA BUCHAN

Flemington by Violet Jacob was recommended to me by my grand-parents. Posthumously. When writing my biography of John Buchan, I came across a letter he wrote in 1911 to the author, soon after the book was published: 'My wife and I are overcome with admiration for [*Flemington*] and we both agree that it is years since we read so satisfying a book. I think it the best Scots romance since *The Master of Ballantrae*. The art of it is outstanding.'

In the normal run of things I'm a sucker for a Jacobite tale, even if Bonnie Prince Charlie makes me weep with frustration, but I admit I was nervous before opening the book, since I found *The Master of Ballantrae* unendurably upsetting and bleak. I need not have worried. *Flemington* is a powerful, affecting drama, as you would expect of any 'romance' of the '45, but it is not hopeless. And, although all the characters are flawed, in three of them there is something of distinction, even nobility.

The book begins with an account of juvenile naughtiness by the 'hero', Archie Flemington, through whose eyes we see much of the action. He is half-Scots, half-French, a mercurial being full of charm and mischief with a talent for painting, who is brought up by his adored but stern and manipulative grandmother, Christian Flemington, in a remote country house called Ardguys in Angus. We meet him next eighteen years later, in the summer of 1745, when he

Violet Jacob, *Flemington* (1911)
Association for Scottish Studies · Hb · 238pp · £9.95 · ISBN 9780948877230

insinuates himself into the graces of a vain, boobyish, retired judge called Lord Balnillo, in an imposing house of the same name over-looking the South Esk estuary near Montrose.

We gradually learn that Archie Flemington is a government agent who has been told to spy on Balnillo's much younger brother, a sol-dier of fortune called Captain James Logie and a known Jacobite. Archie's job is to find out what James Logie is up to. He follows him discreetly at night, to the back streets and quays of Montrose, where he discovers him plotting with another notorious Jacobite called Ferrier. The next morning, James meets Archie by chance on a hill-side near Balnillo. Archie reminds James powerfully of his dead wife, and, though normally a buttoned-up action man, he blurts out the story of her betrayal and death in the Netherlands. Believing Archie to be a Stuart sympathizer James promises to help him if he gets into difficulty, giving him the names of two safe houses and offering him money if he needs it. Archie feels such an affinity with James (one might almost say that he falls in love with him) that he vows never to betray him. Thus is the tragedy set in motion.

Archie flees Balnillo and heads home to Ardguys, to tell his grand-mother of his decision not to go after James Logie. Christian Flemington is an extraordinary woman of haughty dignity and high intelligence, luminously described, who is eaten up with bitterness at the treatment that she and her son received in France from the mother of King James III (better known, in England at least, as 'The Old Pretender'). She had brought up her grandson to hate the Jacobite cause as much as she does and had persuaded him to become an agent for King George II. As Violet Jacob puts it: 'There was only one fitting place for him, and that was in the hollow of her hand.'

The reader is confronted with the customary slippery half-truths, treachery and brutality that disfigured both sides in that conflict: an uneven conflict, since one side still cleaved to a species of medieval feudalism, while the other was more forward-looking, if thoroughly unsympathetic. But, in this novel, the conflict is seen mainly from the Whig side, which is unusual and, I must say, refreshing. Moreover, the strongly Jacobite east coast of Scotland rarely gets a look in in this kind of fiction, perhaps because it's not so picturesque as the Highlands.

Archie's refusal to hunt down James Logie and thus, in effect, shield a considerable 'rebel', causes his grandmother to revile him as a turncoat and cast him off, at least temporarily. Distraught, he devises a plan to go back to Montrose to warn the captain of the government sloop, the *Venture* – without implicating James – that the Jacobite forces, led by Logie and Ferrier, are going to attack. He witnesses that attack, but as luck would have it, comes across James on the island of Inchbrayock; the latter realizes with horror that Archie has betrayed him, and they fight. Archie is injured, but James is urgently called elsewhere before he can finish him off.

In the end, Archie is denounced as a traitor by another well-drawn character, Skirlin' Wattie, a crippled beggar and balladeer, who acts as a postman for government spies, and who overhears Archie speak of James and how he can trust him, when delirious with fever after his fight on Inchbrayock. But such are the shifting sands which everyone had to navigate in times of civil war, that we understand Wattie's motivation perfectly. I won't spoil it by describing the climax of the tale; suffice it to say that those who need most to know that Archie is essentially an honourable man are not left wondering.

Violet Jacob very cleverly wove together fact and fiction. She was deeply attached to the Angus landscape, which she describes beautifully, having been brought up at the House of Dun (on which Balnillo is based) as a member of an ancient family called Kennedy-Erskine. The house now belongs to the National Trust for Scotland and may be visited. If you do not know the area around Brechin and Montrose, it is worth keeping a map by your side when reading the book. I suspect that Violet Jacob would still recognize the country-side a hundred years on; the most substantial change has been to Inchbrayock, just off the southern edge of the Esk estuary, which is no longer an island, the narrow channel having been filled in many years after the book was published.

She describes actual events, in particular the capture of the *Venture* (in reality the *Hazard*), anchored off Montrose in November 1745. However, the battle of Culloden the following April is only reported, not described. All the principal characters are fictitious, although she includes a deadly cameo of the boorish, cruel 'Butcher' Cumberland, to whom Christian Flemington applies for mercy to save her grandson. But Violet Jacob is the cleverest of historical novelists; steeped in the history, customs and language of Angus as she was, she created the atmosphere without bludgeoning the reader with detail, as lesser novelists are inclined to do.

The writing is by turns poetic, highly visual (since the countryside is seen through the eyes of the artist, Archie) and sharply direct. There are flashes of dark humour, in particular in the descriptions of the romantic advances the ridiculous Balnillo makes to Christian Flemington. There are telling changes of pace: the scene when Archie stalks the Jacobite plotters through the wynds of Montrose is nerve-janglingly tense. The book also feels, in a strange way, rather modern or, perhaps more accurately, Violet's preoccupations are simply enduring ones. A hundred years ago, homoerotic feeling was not a subject discussed too openly, I imagine, since homosexual acts were considered both a sin and a crime; however, plenty of people had sympathy for the predicament of those drawn strongly to their own sex. Certainly, the attraction that Archie feels for James is too intense to be explained simply by the attractions of male friendship, and it shapes the rest of his life.

Violet Jacob led a far from confined or sheltered life, particularly after her marriage to Arthur Jacob, a professional British soldier, who took her to India and Egypt, as well as to a number of garrison towns in England. As a young, as yet unmarried, woman my grandmother met her in Cairo one winter early in the last century. Years later, she wrote: 'Violet had published a small book of poetry, which made her a little suspect to the military society in Cairo. But her charm and beauty and aptitude for getting on with people helped her to live down even poetry.'

Flemington was not Violet's first novel – *The Sheep-Stealers* and *The Interlopers* are the best known of the others – but it sold the most, and has lasted. However, she never wrote another novel after *Flemington*. My grandmother explained why: 'Violet had one son, whom she loved with all the depth of an imaginative and passionate nature. When he was killed in the 1914 war a spring in her broke. She never wrote a long book again, and turned to writing poems in the Scottish vernacular.'

That 'vernacular' was 'the Doric', the speech of Angus, already in retreat when she wrote *Flemington*, but capable of adding marvellously to the colour of it, and really not difficult for the modern reader to understand. Her best-known book of poems in the vernacular is *The Songs of Angus* (with a preface by John Buchan), published in 1915. Hugh MacDiarmid, the high priest of the Scottish literary renaissance after the First World War, reckoned that she was 'the most considerable of the contemporary vernacular poets'. She also wrote acutely observed short stories set in Angus, collected in *Tales of My Own Country* (1922), as well as a history of her forebears, *The Lairds of Dun*, in 1931. She died in 1946, at Kirriemuir, Angus (J. M. Barrie's birthplace), where she went to live after she was widowed.

The Jacobite 'rebellion' has always attracted the attention of novelists but, Sir Walter Scott and Robert Louis Stevenson apart, there can be few writers who have ever matched Violet Jacob's sure touch with plot, nor her lyrical descriptions, which she yet never allows to get in the way of the action. Tell it not in Gath, but I prefer her take on the Jacobite rebellion to either of theirs, if only because there is so little in *Flemington* about the infuriating Bonnie Prince Charlie.

URSULA BUCHAN writes non-fiction for pleasure rather than profit. You can hear her talking about garden writing on our podcast, Episode 9, 'Well-Cultivated Words'.

Joy Undimmed

MATHEW LYONS

John Masefield was in his last year as Poet Laureate when I was born in 1966. I remember copying out his poem 'Cargoes' in primary school – 'Quinquireme of Nineveh from distant Ophir . . .' – and wondering what all these strange, beautiful-sounding words meant as I laboured over my ascenders and descenders. *That* John Masefield, stiff and distant, seemed already to be from a long-dead past.

So it came as a shock to discover that he was the same John Masefield who wrote *The Midnight Folk*, which seemed to burst from its pages in a torrent of surprises and delights. It was – and is – one of my favourite books, but, while the sheer joy of it is undimmed, I can now see that it stayed in the memory because it is full of deep feelings, and the ultimate resolution of its plot has an emotional satisfaction that I felt as a child but did not then understand.

First published in 1927, *The Midnight Folk* is still in print; but it is less well known than its sequel, *The Box of Delights*, which many remember from a successful BBC TV adaptation in the 1980s. Set in the 1890s, its premise is the staple of much children's literature: a lonely young child, in this case a boy named Kay Harker, has lost his parents and is being brought up by an indifferent guardian and a cruel governess. His great-grandfather, Captain Harker, in whose house Kay lives, lost some treasure – 'church ornaments, images, lamps, candlesticks, reliquaries, chalices and crosses of gold, silver and precious stones' – entrusted to his care by the archbishop of a

John Masefield, *The Midnight Folk* (1927)
Farshore · Pb · 304pp · £8.99 · ISBN 9781405210126

South American port during the revolutions and uprisings of 1811. The loss haunted him until his death, a haunting that also ruined the happiness of his wife and son. Now others more avaricious than Kay are on the treasure's trail. Can he find it before they do? It is only at the end that you realize the book is about the restoration of more than one kind of treasure.

Masefield takes this scenario and stuffs it with every imaginable device of children's literature – talking animals, pirates, hidden passages, invisibility potions, mermaids, King Arthur and more. But he also stuffs it with story itself. Kay hears – or overhears – pieces of the treasure's history from multiple storytellers. You might say the pieces of story are, in their own way, pieces of treasure too. He hears – or remembers hearing – countless stories of local folklore and history from the indefatigable maid, Ellen. These range from rick burners and smugglers to the highwayman Benjamin, who lived in the stables long ago; from the murder victim surely buried under the hearth in Kay's bedroom to the man, known only as The Tailor, found killed in one of the outhouses, 'stabbed right through the skull,' Ellen says with relish, 'which shows you the force that must have been used'. He also hears about other hidden things through his animal friends, the black cat Nibbins, Bitem the fox, Blinky the owl: the secret passageways of the house, the secret ways of a coven of witches, the secret lives of the animals themselves. Kay soaks up every last word. Not for nothing is the Harker crest three *oreilles* couped.

But if *The Midnight Folk* is a book about story, it is also a book about time. It is steeped in the past, layer after layer of it. There are the layers of the treasure story, folded around three generations, but other histories are interleaved everywhere: great floods and storms, the druids, the Wars of the Roses, the reign of Henry VIII, the Battle of Naseby, the plague and so on. And the book is also concerned with the passage of time itself: with the cuckoo clock striking in the night, with church bells and dinner bells, with a repeater watch, which Benjamin hid and Kay now finds, with the decayed clock in the harness room. When two of the book's villains were last seen alive, during the Great Flood of February 1850, they were at the Ring of Bells Inn. When we meet Bert the sexton, he is winding the clock. To what end is all this?

One of Masefield's many narrative tricks is to bring a painting to life. While Kay is talking to the first of these, of Captain Harker, 'A black cat with white throat and paws, which had been ashes for forty years, rubbed up against great grandpapa Harker's legs, and then, springing on the arm of his chair, watched the long dead sparrows in the plum tree, which had been firewood a quarter of a century ago.' Even as Kay is enveloped in the past, he must understand that it is gone. 'Time's lost, done with, but must be paid for,' one of Kay's grandmothers, another of the dead woken from the sleep of portraiture, tells him. Which is another way of saying that the burdens of the past can only be redeemed by the life of the present. The loss of Kay's parents is barely alluded to, but his situation is reinforced on almost every page: adrift without family, he is trapped in every kind of past, in everyone else's stories, with an unreachable future ahead of him. He is in dire need of a 'now' to live in.

Many of the stories within *The Midnight Folk* range freely over the past, but its essential narrative runs over five days and nights that are alike interwoven with action, both natural and supernatural, realized with a dream-like fluidity and brilliance. You quickly lose track of what is day and what is night, what might be dream and what is real. The effect is mesmerizing; it captures better than anything I know the strange, hypnogogic state between sleep and waking when the world itself feels woozily pliant to the near-conscious mind. It is the prose equivalent of a painting by Marc Chagall; remarkably, it even does away with chapters, the narrative slipping like water through the fingers of convention.

It's a surprise, then, to discover that the book contains deep elements of autobiography. *The Midnight Folk*'s premise may be unoriginal, but it's nevertheless one that was deeply real to Masefield himself. His Herefordshire childhood was idyllic; he delighted in the landscape, its sense of place and history, its folklore and its myths. He seems to have been highly attuned to wonder – and to its corollary, terror – sensitivities which were further heightened when he discovered the power of storytelling, both as teller and receiver.

'It is difficult for me to describe the ecstatic bliss of my earliest childhood,' he wrote in a late memoir, *So Long to Learn*:

> All that I looked upon was beautiful, and known by me to be beautiful, but also known by me to be, as it were, only the shadow of something much more beautiful, very, very near, and almost to be reached, where there was nothing but beauty itself in ecstasy, undying, inexhaustible . . .
>
> I was sure that a greater life was near us: in dreams I sometimes seemed to enter a part of it, and woke with rapture and longing. Then, on one wonderful day, when I was a little more than five years old . . . I entered that greater life; and that life entered into me with a delight that I can never forget. I found that I could imagine imaginary beings complete in every detail . . . with an incredible perfection, in a brightness not of this world.

Then, when Masefield was 6, his mother died. He was sent to live with an aunt and uncle who didn't understand him and don't seem to have liked him much either. *The Midnight Folk*, then, is written out of these, Masefield's own remembered desolations, and its gorgeous delight in the power of story to make sense of the world reflects his own experiences of grief and consolation. It is as if a lost boy had conjured his longed-for childhood back to life through sheer force of imagination. The book is not merely a fantasy for children, but an embodiment of a child's capacity to dream – and, ultimately, an argument for the emotional importance of fantasy, of story, itself. You could say it's Masefield's love letter to story; but perhaps it is a letter of thanks too.

At its core, *The Midnight Folk* is about restitution: stolen treasure returned to the church from which it was taken; the watch Benjamin stole restored to its owner's family; restless souls allowed to sleep in peace. And one of the book's most striking characteristics is its empathy. We are invited to empathize with almost everyone. With Captain Harker, his last years swallowed in grief. With the two men who stole the treasure from him, one of whom drank himself to death out of guilt, and the other who set out to undo the wrong he had done and lost his life in the process. We are invited to empathize with Benjamin the highwayman – 'a slight, quick man, with a nice face,' Ellen has heard, 'nothing bad in it, only bold' – and the horse shot from beneath him in the final desperate chase, and with Bitem the fox, who also knows a thing or two about being hunted. We are even invited to empathize with the book's chief villains, the three generations of Americans all known as Abner Brown. One, the grandfather, disappeared in the flood of 1850. 'I've often thought of his people, far away, never knowing,' the sexton tells Kay. 'Though they'll have done sorrowing by now, poor souls.'

But if *The Midnight Folk* is about restitution, its most powerful redemption is quietly told, hidden in the final folds of the action. Poignantly, the agents of it – the heroes who return to restore the world to order – are Kay's childhood toys, long banished by the governess. ('They will only remind him of the past,' Kay overhears her tell Ellen.) How much private sadness did Masefield weave into that idea? Redemption wrapped inside a memory wrapped inside a loss.

And what form does the redemption finally take? A woman steps out of one of Kay's dreams at the book's close to take care of him. 'I am Carolina Louise, who loved your Mother,' Masefield has her tell him. It was, of course, his own mother's name.

MATHEW LYONS is a writer and historian who lives in East London. Thanks to Kay, he still sometimes wonders about tigers under the bed at night.

Through a Glass, Madly

MARTIN SORRELL

In my day, the A-level Spanish syllabus included a few score of the key pages of *Don Quijote* – windmills mistaken for giants, labourers for lords, prostitutes for princesses, and so on. When I got to university I found that we were supposed to know the whole novel. I struggled through most of it but couldn't handle its digressions and longueurs. Cervantes could veer off at tangents and not return for a hundred pages or more. My tutors encouraged me to persevere. After all, Cervantes was revered as Spain's Shakespeare.

These days, I remember little of *The Quixote*, as the literati call it. But what I *do* recall, vividly, is a short story from a collection of twelve which was also on my undergraduate programme. In 1613, three years before he died, Cervantes produced his *Novelas Ejemplares* or *Exemplary Novellas*. Exemplary in the sense of instructive; they're cautionary tales. They're all strong stories, some stronger than others. But one especially has lodged in my memory, and because of the pandemic I've been thinking about it more than usual.

'El Licenciado Vidriera' – 'The Glass Graduate', or, in someone's bright coinage, 'Dr Glass Case' – is the story of a young man who for a while is convinced he's made of glass. He's called Tomás Rodaja. Aged 11, he'd arrived in Salamanca, seat of Europe's third-oldest university, hoping to find service with any master who'd give him the freedom and opportunity to study. Eight years later, aged 19, he's achieved most of his goals. But then an army recruiter charms him with tales of the soldier's life. Tomás accompanies him to Italy. There follow several pages of travelogue, an account of places in Italy which possibly Cervantes knew as a soldier himself. The pair then transfer to Flanders. Eventually, Tomás is drawn back to his original plan of becoming a lawyer. He returns to Salamanca. One day he's introduced to a woman who falls violently in love with him, but he does not love her. Desperate, she slips Tomás a love potion. The result is not lust but lunacy. Tomás falls seriously ill, and on recovering he believes he's made entirely of glass. He's also become a fount of wisdom, dispensing aphoristic pearls to anyone who asks. He's a sort of king's fool, part-Socrates part-circus act. After two years he's cured of his delusion. He changes his name and asks for nothing more than to be left in peace to practise law. It's not to be. People want him only as the dotty man of glass. Disillusioned, he returns to Flanders, where, ironically, he achieves fame as a soldier, dying in battle.

A cautionary tale indeed. Fortune is fickle; one minute you're the toast of the town, the next you're toast. And there's the perennial question: are the mad saner than the rest of us? A question that applies to poor, magnificent Don Quixote, whose story – from sanity to delusion to disenchantment – is Tomás's, if writ much larger.

'The Glass Graduate' was working away at me well before the pandemic brought it into sharp focus again. Around 2005, I decided to write a radio play about the glass delusion, as it's known. I'd found out more about it in bits of my reading. Andrew Solomon mentions it in his monumental book on depression, *The Noonday Demon*, and it's there in Robert Burton's classic *The Anatomy of Melancholy* of 1621.

I wrote my play and the BBC took it on condition they could add two documentary strands: an intermittent commentary by Andrew Solomon; and contributions by glassmakers Mark and Patricia Tranter. My brother Neil composed music which he scored for glass jars, beakers and retorts.

The glass delusion is about human fragility, the unstable ego. It's both a defence mechanism and a threat. Don't touch me or I'll break into little pieces, and you yourself might well be wounded. The delusion was quite common in Cervantes' time, an era, according to Andrew Solomon, when the techniques of manufacturing clear glass were perfected. Here was a unique medium, simultaneously an absence and a presence, a piece of magic, a barrier that could be passed through by light waves (and Alice). Glass is usually our friend; but for a disturbed few, it's a metaphor for damage and extinction. Sufferers from the delusion took extraordinary measures to safeguard themselves. They avoided contact with other people, but if they couldn't, they donned layers of protective clothing. If travel was unavoidable, they'd have themselves packed in straw and carried around in crates or on litters. One man thought his buttocks were made of glass, and so refused ever to sit down.

There were some famous people among the deluded, King Charles VI of France the highest-ranking of them, while Princess Alexandra of Bavaria and Tchaikovsky suffered from closely allied conditions. By the modern era, the delusion had just about died out, though there were a few attested cases in the twentieth century, one as late as the 1940s. Because clear glass has been ubiquitous for centuries, hypochondria – the glass delusion surely comes under that heading – has now found other metaphors which better reflect the threats and realities of the modern age.

But we're all just as fragile as Tomás Rodaja. The latest and grisliest reminder of that inconvenient truth is coronavirus. We've had to behave like the glass graduate, but for the least deluded of reasons. We may not have packed ourselves in straw, but it's as if we did. For straw and padded clothing, read masks and social distancing. Someone's cough or sneeze or accidental nudge could shatter the shell each one of us inhabits, precarious as crystal.

When I first read 'El Licenciado Vidriera', I thought it powerful but anachronistic. When I wrote my play, I thought Cervantes' story relevant and disturbing in ways I couldn't quite fathom. Today, I get it one hundred per cent.

MARTIN SORRELL's *The Glass Man* received the 2006 Mental Health Media Award for the best radio drama.

Bibliography

Coming attractions

BRANDON ROBSHAW opens a box of delights ·
SUE GEE goes boating with Mole and Ratty · JIM
RING doesn't mean to go to sea · PAULINE
MELVILLE sets sail for Guyana · GRANT MCINTYRE
gathers herbs at Copsford · RACHEL COOKE joins
the war between the Tates · ROGER HUDSON
reads the letters of the Lady Stanleys ·
ALEXANDRA HARRIS picks up a Pevsner

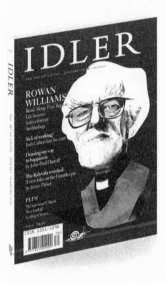
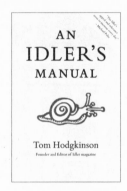